Ebert's Little Movie Glossary

Other Books by Roger Ebert

An Illini Century
A Kiss Is Still a Kiss
Two Weeks in the Midday Sun:
    A Cannes Notebook
Behind the Phantom's Mask
Roger Ebert's Video Companion

With Daniel Curley
The Perfect London Walk

With Gene Siskel
The Future of the Movies:
    Interviews with Martin Scorsese,
    Steven Spielberg, and
    George Lucas

With John Kratz
The Computer Insectiary

Ebert's Little Movie Glossary

A compendium of movie clichés, stereotypes, obligatory scenes, hackneyed formulas, shopworn conventions, and outdated archetypes

by Roger Ebert

*Andrews and McMeel
A Universal Press
Syndicate
Company
Kansas City*

Ebert's Little Movie Glossary
©1994 by Roger Ebert.
All rights reserved.
Printed in the United States of America.
No part of this book may be used
or reproduced in any manner whatsoever
except in the case of reprints
in the context of reviews.
For information write
Andrews and McMeel,
a Universal Press Syndicate Company,
4900 Main Street,
Kansas City, Missouri 64112.

"The Laws of Cartoon Motion" © 1980 by
Mark O'Donnell. Reprinted by kind permission.

Library of Congress Cataloging-in-Publication Data

Ebert's little movie glossary.
        p.   cm.
    Compiled by Roger Ebert.
    ISBN 0-8362-8071-7 : $12.95
        1. Motion pictures—Humor. I. Ebert, Roger.
    II. Title : Little movie glossary.
    PN1994.9.E2   1994
    791.43'0207—dc20   94-26680
                                                    CIP

First Printing, September 1994
Second Printing, March 1995

Designed by Cameron Poulter

This book is for Raven and Emil.

Introduction

You go to enough different movies, you start to notice things. Like how every time there's a chase scene in an exotic locale, a fruit cart gets overturned. Or how whenever the hero knocks out a Nazi sentry and puts on his uniform, the uniform is a perfect fit. Or how there are plots that would be over in five minutes, if all of the characters weren't idiots. These are clearly observations crying out to be organized into *Ebert's Little Movie Glossary*.

Actually, the Idiot Plot started this whole enterprise. It was identified in the 1950s by a science fiction author named James Blish, and it changed forever my way of reading. Maybe it even started me down the road to becoming a critic. It led me to the startling conclusion that I preferred books and movies in which the characters were, for the most part, at least as smart as I was.

The first Glossary appeared in the *Chicago Sun-Times* in the early 1980s. It was expanded for publication in the 1986 edition of my *Movie Home Companion,* and appeared annually until 1993, when it had grown so large it clearly deserved a book of its own. The first definitions were written by me, but then readers and moviegoers started sending in their own contributions, and after the Glossary appeared in my section on CompuServe, they arrived by e-mail, too.* There are now about four hundred entries, some two hundred fifty of them seeing print for the first time in this book.

My thanks go to those brilliant and perceptive contributors, and especially to those so prolific they seem to have embraced

Glossary-writing as a second vocation: Andy Ihnatko, the Macintosh expert; Rich Elias, the film critic; Stuart Cleland, the "Siskel & Ebert" staff guru; and Jeff Levin, the sage of Rochester. Other contributors are from all over the country and from Canada, Australia, Israel, Finland, Switzerland, Puerto Rico, England, the Netherlands, and elsewhere. Friends such as Emo Phillips, the comedian; Billy (Silver Dollar) Baxter, the raconteur; and Donna Martin, the editor, also pitched in; and some of the most valuable contributions (including the immortal Fallacy of the Talking Killer) came from my colleague Gene Siskel.

It was Siskel, too, who once observed, "It's amazing how many movies are not as interesting as a documentary of the same actors sitting around talking over lunch." Sometimes I think the Hollywood system encourages filmmakers to "dumb down" their material. Perhaps this compendium of clichés, stereotypes, obligatory scenes, hackneyed dialogue, and transparent ruses will encourage those brave few who try to make movies at least as smart as they are.

Maybe it will also tip off audiences. One of the proudest moments in my career as a critic came as I sat in a darkened theater and heard a fellow audience member (someone unknown to me) shout out "Fruit Cart!"

Roger Ebert

*We received one e-mail "contribution" too many. The entry entitled "Newton Improved, or, the Nine Laws of Cartoon Thermodynamics" in the first printing of this book was sent to me on the Internet, and I received permission to use it from its "authors"—only to learn after the book was in stores that this amusing piece of comic writing was, in fact, by Mark O'Donnell of New York.
My sincere apologies to Mr. O'Donnell.

Actress Inferior Position. In movie sex scenes, which are usually directed by men, the POV at the moment of climax is almost always the man's, so that we see the actress, not the actor, losing control.

GENE SISKEL

AC-WAT-NOBI Movie. A Cop With A Theory No One Believes In.

ROBERT TARRY GROUCHY, *University of Calgary*

Against All Odds Rule. In an apparently fatal situation from which there is no possible hope of survival, it is certain the characters will survive. In a situation where there is any apparent chance of survival, there will be at least some deaths.

R.R. KUNZ

"Ain't Nobody Here but Us Chickens." Whenever someone is alone at home at night and they hear a sound in the house and ask aloud, "(Name), is that you?" it *never* is.

JAMES PORTANOVA

Air Vent Escape Route. If the hero is imprisoned in a building owned by the villains, there will inevitably be an air vent cover that is not screwed in and is easily removed. The passageway will be large enough to accommodate any size person. The escape route will pass over the room where the bad guys are discussing the details of their diabolical plan, which the hero will now be able to foil.

DONA KIGHT, *Chicago*

Alien Berlitz Communication Rule (ABC Rule). Movie aliens are able to learn the local language (English, French, Japanese, etc.) in an amazingly short time. Frequently this includes the ability to reproduce recognizable Earth-like accents. See also "Universal Translator."

RICHARD ROHRDANZ, *West Kennebunk, Maine*

Ali MacGraw's Disease. Movie illness in which only symptom is that the sufferer grows more beautiful as death approaches.

Animal Kingdom, Sights and Sound Of. (1). In at least one scene in any movie about the "jungle"—no matter where in the world—the sound track must feature the demented call ("*who-who-who-ah-ah-ah-ah-HA-HA*") of an Australian kookaburra (the "Laughing Jackass Bird"). (2). Except when dogs pee on someone's foot for comic effect, animals on film never micturate or defecate. (3). Before 1970, any predatory mammal—wildcat, wolf, or bear—was vicious and bad, deserving to be shot by the good guy. Now they've become noble and powerful—and somehow less carnivorous; perhaps they have discovered tofu.

STEVE W. ZACK, *Nedding, Calif.*

Antiheroine Skin Rule. In a Horny Teenager Movie, the "bad girl" who is the object of the hero's desire will always expose more flesh than the girl whom he ends up with at the end of the film, despite equal sexual activity. If the "good girl" is shown topless in a love scene, it must be accompanied by slow music. In a Dead Teenager Movie, the girl who exposes the least skin is inevitably the only survivor.

JIM O'BRIEN

Animal Kingdom, Sights and Sounds of.

Ark Movie. Dependable genre in which a mixed bag of characters is trapped on a colorful mode of transportation. Examples: *Airport* (airplane), *The Poseidon Adventure* (ocean liner), *Marooned* (space satellite), *The Cassandra Crossing* (train), *Aliens* (outer space), *The Hindenberg* (dirigible), *The Taking of Pelham One Two Three* (subway train), *Abyss* (undersea station), and of course the best of them all, *Stagecoach*.

Asian Grandfather Rule (Yan's Law). All elderly Asians in movies speak in aphorisms like Sydney Toler in the old Charlie Chan movies.

BILL BECWAR, *Wauwatosa, Wis.*

Asian Woman Rule. Any Asian woman with a greater than incidental part in a movie always falls in love with the hero, no matter how big a slob he seems to her (or any other) culture.

BILL BECWAR, *Wauwatosa, Wis.*

Auto Audio Rule. The sound a vehicle makes in a movie chase scene will in no way correspond to any sound made by same vehicle in real life (tires squealing on dirt or around corners at low speed, etc.).

EDWARD SAVIO, *San Francisco*

Automatically Arriving Automobiles. Whenever cars in a chase go through a four-way junction, unrelated cars must appear from each direction and skid into the center. These cars may either stop unharmed or

Ark Movie . . . A Colorful Mode
of Transportation

crash into each other in the center, upon which all the drivers will get out and shake fists at each other. No cars actually involved in the chase are ever involved in the crash.

STEPHEN ROWLEY, *Melbourne, Australia*

Backseat Inviso-Syndrome. Film characters are invariably unable to see a person crouched in the backseat of a car (even a convertible) when, in the real world, it is an impossible place for a person to hide.

ERIC SKOVAN, *Poughkeepsie, N.Y.*

Bad Movie Rental Warning Rule. If a rental movie box has a warning such as "If scenes of graphic horror offend you, do not rent this film!"—do not rent this film.

SAM WAAS, *Houston*

Bad Smoker Rule. In any cop movie made since the mid-seventies, the bad guys smoke, while the good guy is trying to quit.

Baguette Envy. In every scene which includes a person carrying a bag of groceries, the bag will invariably contain a long, skinny, French baguette loaf, and exactly 8.5 inches of it will be exposed.

MICHAEL J. PILLING, *Maple Ridge, B.C., Canada*

Baked Potato People. The nice, good, sweet little people who form a chorus in the hero's background, especially during any movie set in a mental home (cf. *The Dream Team, Crazy People*.) The lesson is always the same: It's the real world that's crazy, and the crazy people who speak real truth. (Inspired by a sign seen by Billy Baxter

Baked Potato People

of New York City on a baked potato in a steak house: "I've been tubbed, I've been rubbed, I've been scrubbed. I'm lovable, huggable, and eatable!")

Balloon Rule. Good movies rarely contain a hot-air balloon. Most egregious use of a hot-air balloon: *Men Don't Leave*, where the heroine is cured of clinical depression by a ride in one. (Readers keep writing in with exceptions to this rule, including *Witness*, but the general principle still applies.)

Balls of Steel Rule. Bad guys who suffer a blow to the groin are down for the count, just like in real life. Good guys shrug it off and are back in action within seconds. See, in particular, *Total Recall*, in which Sharon Stone kicks Schwarzenegger in the groin a half-dozen times within a matter of minutes. Arnold only grits his teeth.

JOHN SNELL

Barroom Bum Slide. Most bar fights in the movies end with the loser being pushed so hard he slides halfway down the bar. In real life, this is impossible.

DOUGLAS W. TOPHAM, *Woodland Hills, Calif.*

Bartender Establishing Shot. All movie bartenders, when first seen, are wiping the inside of a glass with a rag.

DAVID W. SMITH, *Westminister, Calif.*

"Based on a True Story." Hollywood shorthand, meaning: Depressing, morbid, downbeat, including scenes so shocking or

Balloon Rule

lascivious that no producer would include them in a movie unless he could excuse himself by saying these things actually happened.

RICH ELIAS, *Delaware, Ohio*

Bathroom Rule. No one in the movies ever goes to the toilet to perform the usual bodily functions. Instead they either use the bathroom to take illegal drugs, commit suicide, make a criminal deal, kill someone else in a stall, get killed, or sneak out through the bathroom window.

EUGENE ACCARDO, *Brooklyn*

Because They Are There. The top ten lines you can always count on in a mountain-climbing movie: (1). "We have to move fast. We've started late in the season. But if we leave behind the oxygen and most of our equipment and travel light, we can get up there and back before the winter storms." (2). "I know they're still alive." (3). "Leave me here. I can't walk. My legs are broken. By yourself, you have a chance." (4). "Just let me do this one last climb. Then I'll settle down with you and the baby." (5). "Tell them they'll get an extra fifty rupees a day, at the end, if they complete this part of the march." (6). "Sahib! The fresh snow has covered up the crevices! The men say they will go no further today!" (7). "Every previous expedition along this route has had trouble with the porters." (8). "I'd trust him on the other end of my rope." (9). "Take me along. You know I'm a better climber than those guys." (10). "Because it's there."

Because They Are There

Beeping Rule. In movies where cops, reporters, hackers, and others are using a computer to locate a suspect or special file, the successful retrieval of said subject is heralded with dramatic beeps, flashing messages, and other electronic indications that "something important has been found." The only time an ordinary computer ever beeps is when it refuses to carry out a command.

JAMES MOORE, *San Jose, Calif.*

Beginning, The. Word used in the titles of sequels to movies in which everyone was killed at the end of the original movie, making an ordinary sequel impossible. Explains to knowledgeable filmgoers that the movie will concern, for example, what happened in the Amityville house before the Lutzes moved in. Other examples: The First Chapter, The Early Days, etc.

Benevolent Blurbster. A week before a movie opens, all the reviews seem to be ecstatic. Sunday papers and advance TV ads are filled with shouts of unqualified praise, usually attributed to unfamiliar critics from obscure outlets. These "critics" exist primarily for the purpose of supplying such advance quotes, which they are happy to do for the thrill of seeing their names in print. Often they do not even write an actual review, but compose only the blurbs, which they fax or telephone to grateful publicists. Wise moviegoers wait until quotes from real critics from respected sources start appearing in the ads.

Bergman-Allen Hypothesis. Ingmar Bergman regards existential depression as a flaw in the universe. For Woody Allen, it's just hereditary.

RICH ELIAS, Delaware, Ohio

Best Play of the Game Rule. Every bad sports movie ends with the hero making an extraordinary catch/play/hit in slow motion to win the game at the final gun/bell/buzzer.

WEBSTER WATNIK

"Betcha Can't Name That Tune" Ploy. Almost all movie pianists, such as Clint Eastwood in *In the Line of Fire*, are perfectly happy playing nothing but chords. By never straying anywhere near a recognizable melody, they avoid paying royalties.

EMO PHILLIPS, Chicago

***Betsy* Syndrome.** Identifying an actor in print by their latest film, regardless of how weak it was. Inspired by a newspaper article that appeared toward the end of Sir Lawrence Olivier's career, referring to him as "Lawrence (*The Betsy*) Olivier."

BRIAN JONES

Big Lie, The. Refers to all scenes where bad guy paints a beautiful picture and then adds a version of, "One more thing, Benny. I Lied."

MIKE SHEEHAN

Big Nod, The. Comes after the Last Word. After a character is fatally wounded, first he lies motionless and recites an incredibly meaningful statement. Then his head nods to one side.

REX E. RUSSO

Big Wet Dog Shakedown. All wet dogs shake themselves dry only while standing next to well-dressed movie characters.

STEVE WIDEMAN

Birthin' Rule. Any character more than seven months pregnant will give birth by the end of the film, usually in an unusual place, such as an elevator, a cemetery, or the backseat of a car in a traffic jam. The baby is always delivered by someone squeamish and inexperienced who will discover the miracle of life and get the baby named after him/her.

LISA MARTIN, *Toronto*

Black Rock Rule. When a movie starts with the hero arriving in a small town to look up a long lost friend or relative, the person is almost certainly already dead and half the town is in on it. Named for *Bad Day at Black Rock*.

JOE DiCOSTANZO, *New York City*

Blockbuster–Brady Bill Postulate. Since at least one out of every three movie covers at the average video store shows someone holding a gun, you should probably wait at least five business days before renting them.

JEFFREY R. FIELD, *Kansas City*

Body Switch Movie. The brain of one character somehow finds itself in the body of another. Requires actors to confront an actor's nightmare, i.e., acting as if they were another actor.

Bogeyman Shot. Unaware victim is shot in close-up looking toward the camera, while a huge lopsided space is left vacant for the monster/killer to appear in.

PAUL S. WOOLEY, Portland, Oreg.

Boob Tube. There is never anything worth watching on TV in the movies.

JERRY RITCEY

Boom-Boom Rule. Whenever a building or a car explodes, the explosion will be repeated in its entirety from several different camera angles.

SAM CARLSON, Duluth, Minn.

Born in the USA. Any movie set in an un-named U.S. city will be revealed by the credits to have been filmed in Toronto or Vancouver.

R.R. KUNZ

Box Rule. Beware movies advertised with a row of little boxes across the bottom, each one showing the face of a different international star and the name of a character (e.g., "Curt Jurgens as the Commandant"). Example: Most films made from Agatha Christie novels.

Boy-Meets-Girl Rules. If two characters have a Meet Cute, they'll be together by the end of the movie. If they have an antagonistic meet, they'll be together by the middle of the movie.

BARBARA BRIDGES, Los Angeles

Brick Wall Paradox. If a character, while swinging on a rope in an affluent suburb, slams face-first into a brick wall, that character never experiences any injuries other than moaning and sliding off of the wall (e.g., *Home Alone, Cops and Robbersons*).

ROD AHLBRANDT, *Laramie, Wyo.*

British Roman Rule. All leaders of the Roman Empire have British accents. Why don't filmmakers want Romans to at least have Italian accents?

EUGENE ACCARDO, *Brooklyn*

Broken Compass Principle. In New York City chase scenes, cars are able to turn off of avenues onto other avenues. This is impossible, since the avenues are parallel.

DAVID BURD, *East Stroudsburg, Pa.*

Brotman's Law. "If nothing has happened by the end of the first reel, nothing is going to happen." (Named for Chicago movie exhibitor Oscar Brotman.)

Buddy-Brother Road Film. Three-way combo of buddy movie, road movie, and brothers who learn to love each other. E.g., *Coupe de Ville, Rain Man, The Wizard.*

JOHN WECKMUELLER, *Menomonie, Wis.*

Bullet Velocity Rule. In action movies, the speed of a bullet is slowed down enough so that our hero can jump out of the way. In sci-fi movies, the speed of light (lasers/phasers/blasters) is slowed down enough so that the hero/ship can jump/move out of the way and the audience can see the beam moving. The actual formula is: Hollywood

Bullet Speed = (Real Bullet Speed) / (Importance of Character), where the more important a character is, the higher the number.

DAVE EDSON, *Eugene, Oreg.*

***Bullitt* Shift.** Cars in high-speed chases can shift through more gears than they have. Cf. *Bullitt*, where Steve McQueen's car upshifts more than sixteen times.

EDWARD SAVIO, *San Francisco*

Bumbling Night Watchman. Any scene involving the good guy burgling an office at night will inevitably include a semicompetent night watchman, whose sole purpose is to inject an element of danger into an otherwise boring event. Actions performed by the watchman usually include shining a flashlight through the window, rattling doorknobs, watching security monitors, etc., all done in a manner that allows the good guy to continue undetected until just after he discovers the needed information or object. He will then flee the scene with the watchman in pursuit.

RICK NEWBY, *College Place, Wash.*

Bun and Spectacles Rule. Any woman who appears in a movie with her hair in a tight bun and wearing glasses (usually large thick ~nd ones) will inevitably turn out to be ~utiful heroine. She will magically ~rfect vision and a sexy wardrobe.

TOM DRANE

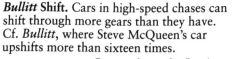

~ory. Every day of the
~s a day, it is possible
~e on cable TV
~e or Gene

Hackman. (Cited in the screenplay for *PCU*, by Adam Leff and Zak Penn.)

Camel, Slow-Moving. All camels in Middle Eastern thrillers are crossing the road for the sole purpose of slowing down a pursuit vehicle.

Camouflage Ramp Certainty Principle. During chase scenes, at least one car will hurtle over a vehicle ramp badly disguised as a normal part of the urban landscape. After flying into the air, the car will usually either strike something and implausibly explode (bad guys) or preposterously survive a landing which should rip the car's suspension to shreds (good guys).

DOUGLAS M. GARROU, *Seattle, Wash.*

Cape Fear **Syndrome.** Derangement that causes heroines, upon learning they are in great danger, to go immediately to an isolated cabin (houseboat, sailboat in the harbor, farm) alone, knowing that no one, especially their friends, will be able to find them.

CHARLES BOOS, *Evanston, Ill.*

Caring Blanket Tuck-In. Effective in conveying the soft heart of an otherwise unappealing character. Cf. James Woods in *Cop.* Also used in scenes involving the hero, usually as a set-up for a scene in which tucked-in child suddenly finds itself in great danger. Cf. Glenn Ford in *The Big Heat.*

TONY WHITEHOUSE, *Verbier, Switz.*

Caring Blanket Tuck-in

Carl Owens Rooftop Spacer. Any male can accurately predict his ability to jump from one rooftop to another. Women jump and end up hanging from their fingernails and being yanked to safety by the guy who jumped seconds before.

BARAK AND ELIZABETH MOORE, *Jerusalem, Israel*

Carphand Tunnel Syndrome. In the movies, hackers who type for upward of ten hours a day are unable to put text on their screens any faster than the average second-grader can read along.

ANDY IHNATKO, *Westwood, Mass.*

Cat Sneeze Effect. In movies, when "silenced" guns are fired, they always make the same sound, resembling a cat sneezing. This is nothing like what any gun, silenced or otherwise, sounds like in real life. Also, no matter how big a gun freak a character is, he always refers to these guns as "silenced." Gun experts in real life call them "suppressed."

RAPHAEL CARTER, *Tempe, Ariz.*

Chain Link Fence Rule. Every alley that the police chase a criminal down ends in a chain link fence that the criminal climbs.

KENNETH C. PARKES

Chase-and-Crash Scenes. Replaces the third act or any other form of plot resolution in the modern thriller. After the hero has left dozens of burning cars and trucks behind him, we never see emergency vehicles responding to the carnage. Despite working under a Wrong-Headed Commanding Officer, (q.v.), the hero cop is never called on the carpet because yesterday he drove his squad car through the walls of several warehouses.

Chirping Computer Syndrome. Computers in movies always make little chirping sounds when characters hit the screen. Computers and terminals haven't made noises like this since the days of the teletype.

FRED CANTWELL, *Ewing, N.J.*

Cinematic Business Pathology Syndrome (CBPS). Affliction that causes sociopathic or criminal behavior by officers of a corporation. Malady is characterized by several symptoms. Look for: (1). company located in a run-down building with a shiny new sign; (2). headquarters in a coldly contemporary building on a corporate campus devoid of people; (3). company sign is plain, rectangular, and flat, with unimaginative artwork; (4). company name includes words like "amalgamated," "consolidated," "-dyne," "-tron," or "chem"; (5). company name includes word "enterprises" following the name of a man who is bald, is fat, or smokes a cigar; (6). company premises are dilapidated while company's owner rides in chauffeured limo.

PAUL A. LEE, *Germantown, Wis.*

Citizen's Band Unbound. When two people in the movies talk over CB or walkie-talkies, 21 they often interrupt each other in the middle of a sentence, as if they were talking on a telephone. This is impossible because the sets receive on the same frequency they broadcast on. See the *Die Hard* movies.

STEPHEN FOOTE, *Barnesboro, Pa.*

Classic Car Rule. Whenever a beautiful classic car—usually the prized possession of an unsympathetic father—is introduced at the beginning of a film, that car will be wrecked by the end of it. (See *Risky Business, Ferris Bueller's Day Off, Coupe de Ville*, etc.)

Clean Up Movie. A motley crew of misfits can't get their act together until a new teacher/coach/nun comes along and straightens them out. Suddenly, they're the best class/team/choir around. Examples: *Summer School, Sister Act* (both parts), *Mr. Baseball, Kindergarten Cop*, etc.

STEVE MYCYNEK, *Des Plaines, Ill.*

Clichéphobia. Condition afflicting people raised on movies. Symptoms arise when real life situations echo movie clichés, and sufferers must take action to avoid what would be the inevitable denouement in a movie. For example: After saying, "Hey, this is the most perfect day of my life," the clichéphobic realizes that such a statement will mean he's dead before the end of the reel. Or, when a last-minute seat unexpectedly opens up on a fully booked airline

Classic Car Rule

flight, the clichéphobic will become convinced that this means the plane is doomed to crash.

MICHAEL MATES AND KATHERINE APPLEGATE,
Sarasota, Fla.

CLIDVIC (Climb from Despair to Victory). Formula for *Rocky* and all the *Rocky* rip-offs. Breaks plot into three parts: (1). defeat and despair; (2). rigorous training, usually shown in the form of would-be MTV videos; (3). victory, preferably ending in freeze-frame of triumphant hero.

Climbing Villain. Villains being chased at the end of a movie inevitably disregard all common sense and begin climbing up something—a staircase, a church tower, a mountain—thereby trapping themselves at the top.

TONY WHITEHOUSE, *Verbie, Switzerland*

Clint Howard Scene. In any Ron Howard movie, the scene where his brother, Clint, makes one of his rare acting appearances (*Backdraft* as the medical examiner, *Far and Away* as the sweat shop foreman, etc.).

DAWSON E. RAMBO, *Pelham Manor, N.Y.*

Clunky Exposition Complex. Fills in vast amounts of background through awkward dialogue. ("You know Betty, we've been married now for five years, and you work in the bean canning factory. I of course have been farming now for all of my life, but despite that, we're still pretty good detectives. I'm sure you remember the assassination of the president of the 4H Club.")

SUZANNE BOOS, Evanston, Ill.

Cocking Principle. When a weaker character is holding a gun on a stronger character who doesn't believe the threat, the weaker character merely has to cock the gun, and the stronger character will back down. Especially effective when small or weak character has to use both hands to cock.

DAVID W. SMITH, Westminister, Calif.

Cole Rule, The. No movie made since 1977 containing a character with the first name "Cole" has been any good. (Exception: *Days of Thunder*, which was good but not all that good.)

Collapsing Display Trick. Pull one can from a pyramid, and they all fall onto the floor. Used by directors who set a scene in a store, and have nothing of substance to achieve there.

Convenient Cat. Any time a good guy is being stealthy and knocks something over, alerting the bad guys, there will be a cat to take the rap. The guard will say, "Ahh, it was just the damned *cat*!" Note that this even works in scenes where a cat has no business being in the first place, such as a museum or computer room.

STEVE WIDEMAN

Cooter Rule, The. When the young, good-looking hero goes back to his boyhood farmhouse, he'll inevitably have a fight at the dinner table with an older, less-attractive brother. The fight is usually about abandoning the farm and "Spitting on Daddy's memory" or the hero's annoying use of correct grammar. The hero storms out of the house and sits down on a fence in the backyard. He is followed by his sweet, long-suffering sister-in-law. She says, "Trap, you're gonna have to forgive Cooter/Hunter/Trip/Billy Bob. He loves you. He don't mean nothin'. It's just his way, is all."

LISA STANSBURY, *Jacksonville, Fla.*

Corrupt Sheriff Rule. All sheriffs who are not the heroes of their movies are corrupt, and in the employ of the largest landowner in the area. Exception: If the sheriff is not corrupt he will be dead by the end of the movie.

JOE DiCOSTANZO, *New York City*

Creeper's Peepers. You can easily spot demonically possessed characters (or actual denizens of Hell) by their glowing red eyes. They seem to switch on involuntarily whenever the characters are alone, in shadow, thinking about how wonderfully evil they are.

MARK J. WOLMERING, *East Hartford, Conn.*

Creeping Doorknob. Any time there is a close-up shot of a doorknob, it will start turning very slowly, and usually without

being noticed by a room's occupants—
unless the occupants are trying to hide, in
which case they will watch in horror as the
knob turns.

RICK NEWBY, College Place, Wash.

Dead Teenager Movie. Generic term for
any movie primarily concerned with killing
teenagers, without regard for logic, plot,
performance, humor, etc. Often imitated,
never worse than in the *Friday the 13th*
sequels. Requires complete loss of common
sense on the part of the characters. Sample
dialogue: "All of our friends have been
found horribly mutilated. It is midnight
and we are miles from help. Hey, let's take
off our clothes, walk through the dark
woods, and go skinny-dipping!"

Dead Werewolf Defense. In any horror film
involving a human transforming into a
monster, the hero never has to explain to
the police the naked dead human body that
is left after he has killed the monster. This
despite the fact that no one in authority ever
believes in the monster in the first place.

JOE DICOSTANZO, New York City

Deadly Change of Heart. When the cold
heart of a villain softens and he turns into a
good guy, the plot will quickly require him
to be killed, usually after maudlin final
words.

Del Close's Rule. Never share a foxhole
with a character who carries a photo of his
sweetheart.

Denim Safety. Ingenious handgun safety mechanism which automatically engages itself when the weapon is jammed into the waistband of a pair of jeans and automatically disengages itself when the weapon is drawn and the muzzle is clear of the actor's naughty bits.

ANDY IHNATKO, *Westwood, Mass.*

Detour Rule. In any thriller, it is an absolute certainty that every road detour sign is a subterfuge to kidnap the occupants of a car. (Cf. Camel, Slow-Moving, "Hay Wagon!" etc.)

Dewey Decimal Dialogue. All conversations set in a library (1). involve at least one exchange between people standing on either side of a shelf and talking to each other through the stacks, and (2). always inspire at least one indignant "Shhhh!" from an elderly librarian. (2a). If a great many books must be carried anywhere in a character's arms, they will be dropped with a loud noise.

Die Three Times Law. In modern movies it has become a law that the villain must die three times. First he gets killed—but isn't really dead! Then he gets killed—but he's still alive. Then he gets killed.

DAVID BURD, *East Stroudsburg, Pa.*

Difficult We Do Immediately, The. Usually happens in the middle of a movie, when the main characters build or repair something which would normally take weeks in about two minutes or less (example: refurbishing a boat which hasn't left the dock in twenty years).

JIM SIMON, *Villa Park, Calif.*

Dirt Equals Virtue. In technology movies, a small, dingy, cluttered little lab and eccentric personnel equal high principles; large, well-lighted facilities mask sinister motives.

PAUL A. LEE, *Germantown, Ohio*

Divine Dog Syndrome. In movies, humans are violently killed with impunity, but dogs are never killed. Thus, an alien race studying films would conclude that dogs are gods.

PAUL CASSEL

"Dr. Curie Will See You Now" Rule. Any time a character's gender is not identified until we have had time to make an assumption, it will turn out to be of the opposite gender. For example, a macho motorcycle rider negotiates a series of obstacles, rides up to the camera, and removes his helmet only to reveal—gasp!—that "he" is a "she!"

BRIAN JONES

Docudrama. TV term for extended-length program which stars a disease or social problem and costars performers willing to give interviews on how they experienced personal growth through their dramatic contact with same.

29

Divine Dog Syndrome

Dog Bites Man Rule. Whenever a character is asked to read an important story in a newspaper, he will inevitably provide a small laugh by reading the wrong story. In movies, no one is capable of scanning a headline and recognizing a story of personal consequence.

PAUL N. YERKEY, *Amherst, N.Y.*

Don't Just Save the Rain Forest—Recycle It! No matter what film you select from the classic Johnny Weismueller "Tarzan" series, one of these sequences will be present: (a) an elephant stampede or (b) Tarzan atop a gigantic crocodile, over thirty feet long, and spinning endlessly over and over as he repeatedly stabs it. These are literally the same sequences lifted in their entirety with new reaction shots of the protagonists dropped in later for continuity.

DAVID H. COLEMAN, *Tarzana, Calif.*

Dorothy Lamour Syndrome. Token female character in a scene with two male leads, is reduced to looking back and forth between the conversing males. Ms. Lamour had an excuse—Hope and Crosby were usually off the script. However, often seen in movies back to the 1940s; in *13 Rue Madeleine* the primary action taken by the lone female spy is to look back and forth in confusion while the two male spies argue just before a parachute jump.

LESA CAMPBELL

Dossier Rule. In a movie where the villain is a rogue CIA/KGB/special forces agent, invariably there is a scene where one of the good guys pulls out a folder stamped "Top

31

Don't Just Save the Rain Forest

Secret." The file contains a blurry photograph of the bad guy (*Apocalypse Now*, *Cliffhanger*). Compare the "Slide Show Rule"—similar, except the head good guy has a magic lantern show, projects a blurry picture of the bad guy, and intones, "He's a former member of the KGB/IRA/Red Brigade" (*Nighthawks*, *In the Line of Fire*).

CHRIS FISANICK, *Barnesboro, Pa.*

Double Step. In an extended dance scene or any other sequence in which a character must demonstrate professional skill, the absurdly simple opening move the actor learns for the close-up before they cut away to the highly trained double's virtuoso performance.

ANDY IHNATKO, *Westwood, Mass.*

Down Under Rule. No film set in Australia is allowed to use the word Australia in its title where "Down Under" is an acceptable alternative. For example, we don't get *The Rescuers in Australia* or *Quigley in Australia*.

STEPHEN ROWLEY, *Melbourne, Australia*

Dramatic Late Arrival Shot. A talented kid has a mother who forbids her to perform. The kid goes on anyway. Just when she's in the spotlight for her big number, the door opens at the back of the auditorium, and who walks in? The mother, of course, who in a later shot inevitably allows herself to relent, smile, and be proud of her kid after all.

Duck Call Shortcut. All waterfowl in TV nature specials make the same sound, regardless of species. It is the sound of a hunter's duck call, and is usually accompanied by the sound of fingers paddling around in water. No matter how much *National Geographic* spends to take pictures of our planet's thousands of duck species, they can't bear to spend more than ten bucks on a sound effect.

RAPHAEL CARTER, *Tempe, Ariz.*

Ellipses Principle. Any film that combines reviewers' quotes with ellipses can't be any good. A review that says "This movie was . . . amazing" probably read "This movie was so awful it is amazing how it ever got made." Reviews of three words or less (e.g., "Funny . . . ," "What a movie . . .") are especially cause for concern.

DAVE KALIN, *San Francisco*

Ellis's Law. A single African-American or Italian in a cast of nonethnic people is usually a good guy. If a film contains more than four African-Americans or Italians in speaking roles, they're all gang members. See *Lethal Weapon* or *My Cousin Vinny* for positives, almost any other film for negatives.

ANDY IHNATKO, *Westwood, Mass.*

Empty Box Syndrome. Any car in a chase approaching a wall of stacked boxes will not only invariably run into it, but will find that the boxes are empty and scatter impressively (which certainly wouldn't happen if boxes labeled, say, "Air Conditioner" were actually full).

STEVEN RAIMI

End Credit Ratio. The longer the end credits are, the more money there was spent on special effects, and the less money there was spent on plot, characterization, and dialogue.

DAWSON E. RAMBO, *Pelham Manor, N.Y.*

Ending, Giving Away the. Critics get hate mail from readers when they reveal too much about the endings of thrillers. Here is the ending of all thrillers: The bad guy gets killed.

RICH ELIAS, *Delaware, Ohio*

Engine Equalization Law. Movie phenomenon which allows large, lumbering Cadillac stretch limousines filled with bad guys to keep up with heroes in exotic sports cars.

EDWARD SAVIO, *San Francisco*

Estrogen Trinity. The Holy Female Trinity in tear-jerking dramas, consisting of: (1). the heroine, who is shy and unsure of her own power as a human being; (2). the mentor, who is brash and outspoken and helps heroine acquire those same qualities; and (3). the corpse, the mother/daughter/sister/friend who announces during dinner that she's been diagnosed with a terminal illness and has less than three reels to live, who helps each of the others achieve perspective and maybe cop an Oscar for the funeral scene.

ANDY IHNATKO, *Westwood, Mass.*

"Everyone's Talking" Rule. If a movie ad portrays happy theater patrons exiting the movie and extolling the film's virtues, the movie itself will invariably be terrible.

DOUGLAS M. GARROU, *Seattle, Wash.*

Explosion ESP. The characters always know whether the crashed and smoldering vehicle they are in will explode. If they don't get out and run, it won't explode. If they do, it does.

KYLE L. CAIN, *Sugar Land, Tex.*

EZ Open Gift Rule. Any time a gift-wrapped present is unwrapped in a movie, it's always easily opened by lifting a separately wrapped lid.

KYLE L. CAIN, *Sugar Land, Tex.*

Factory Confrontation (similar to the Far-Off Rattle Movie). The final battle between the hero and the villain must take place in a factory or stockyard, preferably one with lots of heavy machinery or fire or molten materials. Examples include the *RoboCop, Lethal Weapon,* and *Terminator* pictures.

DAVE KALIN, *San Francisco*

Fallacy of Elaborate Death Techniques. Any method of attempting to kill someone in a movie that is more complicated than shooting, beating, strangling, etc. will inevitably fail. Cf. James Bond's many escapes.

STEVE HORNE

Fallacy of the Predictable Tree. The logical error committed every time the good guy is able to predict exactly what the bad guy is going to do. For example, in *First Blood,* law enforcement officials are searching the woods for John Rambo. A cop pauses

Fallacy of the Predictable Tree

under a tree. Rambo drops on him. Question: Out of all the trees in the forest, how did Rambo know which one the guy would pause under?

Fallacy of the Talking Killer. The villain wants to kill the hero. He has him cornered at gunpoint. All he has to do is pull the trigger. But he always talks first. He explains the hero's mistakes to him. Jeers. Laughs. And gives the hero time to think his way out of the situation, or be rescued by his buddy. Cf. most James Bond movies.

GENE SISKEL

Falling Chess Board Phenomenon. In any movie about a chess fanatic, the chess board that is perpetually set up in his office will always get knocked over by the end of the movie.

DOUG FLETCHER, *Mesa, Ariz.*

Falling Villain, The. At the end of virtually every action-adventure movie, the villain must fall from a great height onto a hard surface. If possible, the villain should crash backward through a plate glass window and land on an automobile.

STEPHEN D. DARGITZ, *Ann Arbor, Mich.*

False Relaxation Reflex. If the film's top villain places his hand on a henchman's shoulder (very important) and tells him not to worry about having screwed up, the henchman will be dead in less than a minute of screen time.

JASON MOORE

Far-Off Rattle Movies. Movies in which the climactic scene is shot in a deserted warehouse, where far-off rattles punctuate the silence.

Fast Food Rule. Wanna know what the summer's blockbuster is going to be? See who McDonald's does the marketing tie-in with. Wanna know what blockbuster will do disappointing business? See who Burger King ties in with.

DAWSON E. RAMBO, *Pelham Manor, N.Y.*

Fat Man Formula. In all movies where groups of men live together, it is always the fat one who cannot be trusted. (See *No Escape*.)

Feedback Rule. Every time anyone uses a microphone in a movie, it feeds back.

ARDEN J. COOPER, *Warren, Mich.*

Feline Fright. When a movie hero/heroine is wandering down any dark and deserted alley, he/she will inevitably be frightened by a cat before encountering the villain.

DAVE KALIN, *San Francisco*

Female Shoot and Cry Rule. Except in movies where the lead is a tough female, any female character who shoots the bad guy for any reason will then drop the gun, bend at the knees, and start sobbing.

GREG BARNARD

Fifty-five-gallon Drum Rule. Fifty-five-gallon drums are a culturally rooted symbol of evil, because they usually contain a substance with a long name that we can't identify. The more drums, the more evil.

PAUL A. LEE, *Germantown, Wis.*

First Law of Funny Names. No names are funny unless used by W.C. Fields or Groucho Marx. Funny names, in general, are a sign of desperation at the screenplay level. See "Dr. Hfuhruhurr" in *The Man With Two Brains*.

First Rule of Repetition of Names. When the same names are repeated in a movie more than four times a minute for more than three minutes in a row, the audience breaks out into sarcastic laughter, and some of the ruder members are likely to start shouting "Kirsty!" and "Tiffany!" at the screen (Cf. *Hellbound: Hellraiser II*).

First Time's the Charm. Ninety-nine percent of sex scenes show couples coupling for the first time.

NIGEL SEARLE, *Venice, Fla.*

Five Minute Class, The. No scene showing a class in session ever lasts more than five minutes. Even the most stimulating session is invariably interrupted by the bell.

DENNIS WARD

Flint Content in Metal. During sword fights, showers of sparks are produced whenever the weapons clang into each other.

MARK J. WOLMERING, *East Hartford, Conn.*

Floating Luggage. In every scene where actors carry luggage, the luggage is obviously empty. They attempt, with pained expressions on their faces, to pretend the bags are heavy, and yet they can flick them around like feathers.

TOM KIRKPATRICK, Chicago

"Food Fight!" Dialogue which replaced "Westward ho!" as American movies ended the long frontier trek and began to look inward for sources of inspiration.

Four Glass Movie. Any movie with a plot that can be summarized on four souvenir soft drink containers from McDonald's. (See also Fast Food Rule.)

Four-to-Three Keyboard Rule. When the camera is focused on a computer screen, it takes four keyboard clicks to produce every three characters.

JIM COLLIER, Dallas

Friendly Fire Tabu. Inevitably, in an action film, a situation will arise where the protagonist almost shoots his partner or is nearly shot by him. Of course, the trigger is never pulled, and the target is recognized as "friendly" just milliseconds before firing, even though visibility is poor, the partner appears on the scene totally unexpected and possibly in disguise, and is pointing a loaded gun! Typically, the two parties have some personal beef with one another that won't be resolved until a later scene.

ROBERT BEMBEN, Ann Arbor, Mich.

Front Row Formula. The character playing the leading role in a movie *always* stands in front of a group of people, for example in an aerobics lesson.

BOB LEFEVERE

Frozen Family Phenomenon. Applies to movies such as *Homeward Bound*, in which the family has lost a minimum of three pets. Family stands looking toward the hill as they think they hear barking. One pet comes over the hill. No one moves. Instead of running toward the hilltop to see if the next pet will appear, the family remains motionless as the second pet arrives. Then family remains frozen until, after suspenseful delay, finally the third pet appears. Arrival of third pet gives permission for family to leap into motion.

LINDA TILLMAN, *Atlanta*

"Fruit Cart!" An expletive used by knowledgeable film buffs during any chase scene involving a foreign or ethnic locale, reflecting their certainty that a fruit cart will be overturned during the chase, and an angry peddler will run into the middle of the street to shake his fist at the hero's departing vehicle.*

"Fruit Cart!" (James Bond Variation). In Bond movies, chase scenes not only upset applecarts, but Agent 007 also invariably plows whatever vehicle he is piloting through the buffet table at an outdoor wedding reception. This is a commentary of

---

*(Of all the definitions in the glossary, this has become the most popular. It has been gratifying to be part of an audience where people unknown to me have cried out "Fruit Cart!" at appropriate moments. The movie *Ski Patrol* even contained a "Siskel and Ebert Fruit Cart.")

Bond's attitude toward monogamy (at least until *Licence to Kill*, when a chase scene ended with Bond parachuting into a DEA agent's wedding to serve as best man.)

ANTHONY BRUCE GILPIN, *Riverside, Calif.*

Fudd Flag. In the background field of an animated cartoon, the one slightly differently painted object (floorboard, cupboard door, rock) among a dozen otherwise identical background objects. This is so Bugs Bunny will know which floorboard his rabbit hole is under, Tom will know which cupboard he'll have to open in order to be bludgeoned by Jerry with a frying pan, and Wile E. Coyote can unerringly choose to cling to the most break-offable piece of rock on the cliff face.

ANDY IHNATKO, *Westwood, Mass.*

Geek Ego Effect. Exemplified by the Dennis Nedry character in *Jurassic Park*, this describes the maniacal behavior of the mandatory nerd with thick glasses, pocket protector, and an I'll-get-even-with-the-rest-of-the-world-for-not-taking-me-seriously attitude.

FRED DECKER

Gender Offender Temporal Paradox. In films set in the present, male characters act like they're from several eras in the past and get punched out by women afterward as a direct result. In films set several eras in the past, female characters act like they're from the present but never get punched out afterward as a direct result.

ANDY IHNATKO, *Westwood, Mass.*

43

Generation Squeeze. Hollywood genre which tries to bridge the generation gap by creating movies which will appeal to teenagers at the box office and to adults at the video rental counter. Typical plot device: An adult becomes a teenager, or vice versa (cf. *Like Father, Like Son*; *Hiding Out*; *Peggy Sue Got Married*; *Vice Versa*; *18 Again*; *Big*). Also sometimes masquerades as a movie apparently about adults, but with young actors in the "adult" roles (cf. *No Man's Land*, *The Big Town*).

Ghost-Repellent Realtor. Even though ghosts desperately want to keep anyone from occupying the houses they haunt, they never bother to show up until the new owners have signed on the dotted line. Since rattling chains during the open house would save them a lot of trouble, it is obvious ghosts are repelled by realtors.

RAPHAEL CARTER, *Tempe, Ariz.*

Gibson's Inverse Coefficient of Gravity. Force of nature which affects firearms of good guys as they scale tall buildings. Force grows geometrically greater the higher up the good guy is, eventually causing firearm to fall irretrievably from his grasp when he needs it most. (Fun Fact: This force generates a powerful visual aura, causing good guy to waste precious time watching firearm fall all the way to the ground while he's in immediate peril.)

ANDY IHNATKO, *Westwood, Mass.*

Godot Movie. Movie in which the producers think that if they just put some big-name comic actors in an oddball situation, something funny is bound to happen eventually. ("Robin Williams, Whoopi Goldberg, and Bette Midler as space pirates!") The audience sits through the whole production waiting for laughs that never come.

ANDY IHNATKO, *Westwood, Mass.*

Gotham Sentence. When a character learns the hero's secret identity, one of two standard movie punishments will result: (a) death or (b) sex with the hero.

ANDY IHNATKO, *Westwood, Mass.*

Gradually Gathering Guffaw. The setup: A bad guy, surrounded by henchmen, is confronted by the hero, who insolently insults him. There is a pregnant pause, during which instant violence seems likely. Cut to: the villain, who pauses for two beats, and then laughs. Cut to: his top henchman, who glances at the boss, waits two more beats, and then laughs, too. Cut to: all the other bad guys, joining in the laughter. (Alternate close: The villain cuts his laugh short and inflicts unexpected pain upon either the good guy or one of his own henchmen.)

Grafik Artz. Banner, sign, or any other handmade drawing which purportedly has been made by untrained hands but which obviously was the expensive work of professional artists. Use of Grafik Artz is usually betrayed by the perfect lines, circles and randomly reversed letters in a child's drawing, or a picket sign at an "impromptu" grass-roots rally which is silkscreened in two-color Dom Casual.

ANDY IHNATKO, *Westwood, Mass.*

Grave Talk. Handy screenwriter's tool where a character can reveal his personality and motivation by explaining everything to a tombstone.

PHIL HEINK, *Lexington, Ky.*

Haircut Hierarchy Rule. The main character in a movie centering around the military or prison never has the same severe crew cut that the other characters have, even though there is usually the obligatory haircut scene. (See Matthew Broderick in *Biloxi Blues*, Tom Cruise in *Top Gun*, Robert Redford in *Brubaker*.)

JIM RACHEFF

Half Nude Rule. People in movies *always* undress from the top down. Especially women.

BILL BECWAR, *Wauwatosa, Wis.*

Hand-in-Hand Rule. In many Hollywood action pictures, the woman characters are incapable of fleeing from danger unless dragged by a strong man, who takes the woman's hand and pulls her along meekly behind him. This convention is so strong it appears even in films where it makes no sense, such as *Sheena*, in which a jungle-woman who has ruled the savage beasts since infancy is pulled along by a TV anchorman fresh off the plane.

Hangman's Eye View. When someone is going to be hung, the shot will start with a view of the crowd, then zoom back to show

46

Hand-in-Hand Rule

that the audience is looking through the noose hanging on the scaffold. (See *Robin Hood, Prince of Thieves*.)

MICHAEL P. FAETH

Hardest Word in the English Language. No matter how well a foreigner speaks English, he will never be able to master "yes," and will invariably be forced to rely on its equivalent in his native tongue.

EMO PHILLIPS, *Chicago*

Harrison Door. Special automated door or barrier, ostensibly designed for high security but which nonetheless moves into place slowly and methodically instead of swiftly and efficiently, thus allowing the escape of celebrities. Harrison Doors are equipped with special sensors triggered by personal charisma, which explains how the hero of a picture set on a crippled undersea vessel manages to squeak past the automatically closing emergency watertight hatch while his comrades drown just behind him. (Named for Harrison Ford, who, whether in danger of being trapped by a thousand-year-old stone door fifty years ago in South America or by a set of bullet-proof doors today in Chicago, has always been its single biggest beneficiary.)

ANDY IHNATKO, *Westwood, Mass.*

"Hay Wagon!" Rural version of "Fruit Cart!" (q.v.). At the beginning of chase scenes through colorful ethnic locales, knowledgeable film buffs anticipate the inevitable scene in which the speeding sports car will get stuck on a narrow country lane behind a wagon overloaded with hay.

Hey! Cody! Rule. Bad guy has drop on good guy. Can pull trigger and kill him. Inevitably shouts "Hey! Cody!" (fill in name of good guy), after which good guy whirls, sees him, and shoots him first.

Hollywood Car. Looks like a normal automobile, but backfires after being purchased from used car lot by movie heroine who is starting out again in life and is on her own this time.

Hollywood Cigarette. In action thrillers where the hero smokes, he only lights one up to snap it angrily away after one or two puffs. (See Bruce Willis in *The Last Boy Scout* and Nick Nolte in *48 HRS* and *Another 48 HRS*, among countless others.)
DAWSON E. RAMBO, *Pelham Manor, N.Y.*

Hollywood Cop Car. Driven by the slovenly member of the team in all police versions of the Opposites in Collision plot. Always unspeakably filthy, dented, rusty, and containing all of the cop's possessions in the backseat, as well as several weeks' worth of fast-food wrappers. Usually, but not necessarily, some kind of distinctive make or model (Gremlin, old Ford woody wagon, beat-up Caddy convertible, 4 x 4 van, etc.).

Hollywood Flavor of the Month. Compulsion by studios to cast the hottest actor of

49

the moment in a coveted role, regardless of whether the actor conforms to the look or style the original author had in mind for the character. (Example: In Avery Corman's novel *Oh God!* the hero is a paunchy, balding, middle-aged Jewish freelance reporter from New York City. In the movie, this character is turned into a WASP supermarket employee from Long Beach, Calif., played by John Denver.)

ANTHONY BRUCE GILPIN, *Riverside, Calif.*

Hollywood Grocery Bags. Whenever a scared, cynical woman who never wants to fall in love again is pursued by an ardent suitor who wants to tear down her wall of loneliness, she will go grocery shopping. The bags will always break, either (1). to symbolize the mess her life is in, or (2). so that the suitor can help her pick up the pieces of her life and her oranges.

CINDY L. CUP CHOY, *Honolulu, Hawaii*

Hollywood Hospital. Where people go to die. Victim checks in, doesn't check out, because screen time is too valuable for characters to go into the hospital only to recover a few scenes later. Dialogue clue: When any seemingly able-bodied character uses the word "doctor," especially in a telephone conversation not intended to be overheard, he/she will be dead before the end of the film.

GENE SISKEL

Hollywood Television. When a TV is part of the set dressing, but is not integral to the plot, the chances are good that it will be playing a Western in black and white, just before or during the cavalry charge, complete with Indian war cries and bugles. The chances of this being true approach 100 percent if (a) the character watching the TV is a cop, (b) he/she is waking up at three in the morning, following (c) a drunken binge after losing his partner, his badge, his wife, or all of the above.

DAWSON E. RAMBO, *Pelham Manor, N.Y.*

Honor Code Rule. In any movie set in either a military academy or a prep school, if the school's "Honor Code" is mentioned within five minutes of the opening credits, it is required that the hero will have to violate the code, motivated by a higher morality, and then: (a) The school officials will begin proceedings to expel the hero; (b) his friends will all look guiltily the other way; (c) the school will come to see the hero's point of view; or (d) his friends will come to his support. (See *The Lords of Discipline*, *School Ties*, *Taps*, *Scent of a Woman*, etc.)

DAWSON E. RAMBO, *Pelham Manor, N.Y.*

Horny Teenager Movie. Any film primarily concerned with teenage sexual hungers, usually male. Replaced, to a degree, by Dead Teenager Movies (q.v.), but always popular with middle-aged movie executives, who like to explain to their seventeen-year-old starlets why the logic of the dramatic situation and the teachings of Strasberg require them to remove their brassieres. (Cf. *Blame It on Rio*, *She's Out of Control*.)

Human Antennae. Movie characters who have an amazing ability to turn on the TV precisely at the moment when a newscaster begins a report on something directly relating to them.

JEFFREY GRAEBNER

Hunter's Walk. Whenever the hero enters an unknown dangerous place, he spends so much time looking behind him, lest he get jumped from the rear, that he ends up walking backward, and backs into the thing he's looking for. (See Kirk's search of Regula One in *Star Trek II* or any Dead Teenager Movie).

JAMES M. CURRAN, *Bloomfield, N.J.*

Idiot Plot. Any plot containing problems which would be solved instantly if all of the characters were not idiots.

Originally defined by JAMES BLISH.

Ihnatko's First Law of Egress. When you begin to notice and anticipate the little circles in the upper right corner of the frame signaling time for a reel change, it's time to see if you can sneak into another theater at the multiplex.

ANDY IHNATKO, *Westwood, Mass.*

Ihnatko's Law of Voice Recognition. A computer sufficiently advanced to allow real-time voice communication between itself and a human will nevertheless speak like a drunk who has just received a serious blow to the head.

ANDY IHNATKO, *Westwood, Mass.*

Impalement Principle. Whenever a sharp object is even remotely hinted at on the screen, someone will be impaled on it. Examples include *Ricochet*, *Red Rock West*, and *Dead Again*.

DAVE KALIN, *San Francisco*

Impregnable Fortress Impregnated. Indispensable scene in all *James Bond* movies and many other action pictures, especially war films. The IFI sequence begins early in the picture, with long shots of a far-away fortress and Wagnerian music on the sound track. Eventually the hero gains entry to the fortress, which is inevitably manned by technological clones in designer uniforms. Sequence ends with destruction of fortress, as clones futilely attempt to save their marvelous machines. (See *The Guns of Navarone*, etc.)

Inevitable Microfiche Library Scene. A tired visual cliché frequent in mystery thrillers, typically rendered in shot/reverse shot fashion: first shot an intense close-up of the whirring blur of the microfiche view screen that suddenly locks onto a crystal clear picture or article; second shot the face of the shocked protagonist—suspicions confirmed! (See *Sliver*, with Sharon Stone watching the whirring microfiche, until it locks onto the photo of the sliver building used throughout. Cut to: her stunned reaction.)

DAVID H. COLEMAN, *Tarzana, Calif.*

Inevitable Sister. In any movie where the heroine catches her boyfriend dancing in public with another woman, and makes a big scene, the other woman invariably turns out to be the boyfriend's sister. (Cf. *Mystic Pizza*, etc.)

STUART CLELAND, *Chicago*

Info-on-Demand. Whatever event the character is concerned or worried about (the killer on the loose, the police man-hunt, the unusual disk-shaped lights in the sky, etc.), when the character turns on the radio or TV, there is an immediate news bulletin that provides full details of the event in question.

MIKE BACHERT, *Columbus, Ohio*

Instant Ignition Rule. In an action movie, any car driven by bad guys that crashes will inevitably explode, with flames instantly filling the passenger compartment, just as though they were carrying open cans of gasoline in their laps. This also happens whenever a car occupied by bad guys begins to fall over a cliff, even before the car has hit anything.

SAM WAAS, *Houston*

Intelligence. In most movies, "all that separates us from the apes." In *Sheena, Queen of the Jungle*, what we have in common with them.

Intelligent Universal Operating Systems. All computers in the movies use the same amazingly powerful operating system that accepts plain English commands. A character simply types OPEN PRIMARY FILE or ACCESS SECURITY SYSTEM. The computer immediately responds. Such computers are always connected to a massive global network, and can access any private file anywhere in the world. In addition, this operating system uses a gigantic, blocky font that is usually bright green on a black background, apparently for the benefit of visually impaired users.

JIM COLLIER, *Dallas*

Inverse Law of Combat Intensity. The intensity of combat in battle scenes is in inverse proportion to distance from the camera. The guys in the foreground usually at least *try* to look like they *may* want to hurt each other, but if you look in the far background you'll see "combatants" just kind of fanning each other with their swords. Extremely popular in, but not limited to, all Italian "sword and sandal" movies.

CHARLIE AMBROSI

Invisible Ceiling. Anyone can climb to the ceiling of a warehouse or practically anything else and not be seen by anyone walking beneath. In a subset of the Fallacy of the Predictable Tree, if the good guy is hiding on or in the ceiling, the bad guy will pause directly underneath so the good guy can fall on him and overpower him. (See *Sneakers.*)

DONA KIGHT, *Chicago*

Invisible Protective Shield. Protects characters during fight scenes. They get hit by fists, chairs, bottles, etc. and thrown through walls, doors, glass, but wear only a small bandage in next scene, and later have no marks, although they should be black and blue for the rest of the movie.

CATHERINE WENT

It's a Black Thing Maneuver. Used when hero needs help or information, and has been refused by rigid bureaucracy. Just as he's leaving in defeat, he is called aside by an employee of the place who is of the same race/nationality/age/ethnicity as the hero, and who breaks the rules by quietly telling him what he needs to know.

MICHAEL E. ISBELL

"It's Over." Whenever a man and woman have narrowly escaped a series of deadly events, the man inevitably says to the woman, "It's over." She then nods gratefully. (See *Seeing-Eye Man*.)

MICHAEL J. PILLING, *Maple Ridge, B.C., Canada*

Joel Silver Rule. All women in action-adventure flicks are extraneous to the plot unless naked or dead.

JIM O'BRIEN

Joel's Observation. Directors always make sure that air ducts are big enough to crawl around in.

First noted by JOEL ROBINSON
of "Mystery Science Theater 3000."

Jolly Bornday. Any obviously concocted song sung during a birthday party scene, chosen so the producers could avoid paying the royalty fees for "Happy Birthday."

ANDY IHNATKO, *Westwood, Mass.*

Joy of Ex. If a cop's daughter or wife is seen in the first twenty minutes of a film, she will be either dead or kidnapped within the next hour. Corollary: If the wife is estranged, her safety is assured; by Hollywood law, the movie cannot end until the cop rescues her and they realize that Maybe They Belong Together After All.

ANDY IHNATKO, *Westwood, Mass.*

Kevin Kline Mustache Principle. When Kevin Kline is sporting facial hair he must play an eccentric, offbeat goofball (*A Fish Called Wanda, I Love You to Death, Soapdish*). To play a serious role he must be clean-shaven (*Dave, Sophie's Choice, Grand Canyon, Cry Freedom*).

ERIC SKOVAN, *Poughkeepsie, N.Y.*

Kidding Battery. In horror films, when the hero/heroine jumps in a car while being pursued by the killer, the car never starts at the first crank. The following generic montage is used: Close-up shot of hero/heroine's face sweating. Face goes out of focus as background focuses to reveal killer approaching car. Close-up of ignition failing again to start engine. Repeat sequence as many times as necessary to match generic crescendo music. Finally, battery gives enough juice to start engine just a second before killer gets the would-be victim. Obviously, the battery was just kidding.

RAYMOND SALFITI

Kinetic Energy Amplification Phenomenon. In scenes involving gunplay, the kinetic energy of the bullets will be enormously amplified as they strike the victim, enabling him to be hurled great distances and through objects. This phenomenon is particularly common around windows and balconies, especially in high-rise buildings.

DENNIS WARD

Kinetic Energy Distortion Phenomenon. When someone is shot while standing near a window, balcony, or ledge, the kinetic energy will always be distorted so as to throw him *outward*, regardless of the direction the bullets came from. This enables victims to be hurled out a window and into a spectacular plunge even if the shots came from outside to begin with.

DENNIS WARD

Kirk Method of Time Management. Regardless of the time a subordinate says will be needed to fix a problem, the supervisor will cut the time by half, at least. Example: Scotty: "I'll need at least twenty minutes to repair the warp drive, Captain!" Captain Kirk: "You've got exactly ten minutes before the *Enterprise* is pulled into the Sun, Mr. Scott!"

ROBERT JONES, *Tigard, Oreg.*

Kojak Moment. In thrillers where the hero is befuddled by an assortment of completely unrelated suspects and victims, the scene in which he suddenly discovers a vacation photo of all of them in a big, grinning group pose.

ANDY IHNATKO, *Westwood, Mass.*

Kookalouris. Name for a large sheet of cardboard or plywood with holes in it, which is moved back and forth in front of a light to illuminate a character's face with moving light patterns. Popular in the 1930s; back in style again with the movies of Steven Spielberg, who uses a kookalouris with underlighting to show faces that seem to be illuminated by reflections from pots of gold, buckets of diamonds, pools of fire, pirate maps, and radioactive kidneys.

Land Boom Rule. In any movie where there is a cocktail party featuring a chart, map, or model of a new real estate development, a wealthy property developer will be found dead inside an expensive automobile.

Last Grab Rule. People pushed off balconies always hang on to the balcony or the person who pushed them for a few seconds before inevitably plunging to their death. Their clutching hand is always pictured in a close-up. (Used twice in *Poison Ivy*.)
SCOTT DALZIEL

Law of Canine/Feline Superperception. Household pets can unerringly detect and react to the presence of ghosts, aliens, or other nonhuman entities. Their warnings are invariably ignored.
DEREK WOOD, *Palo Alto, Calif.*

Law of Colorful Chemicals. In scenes set in any kind of laboratory, there are always lots of flasks filled with lots of bright, colorful chemicals—red, blue, green—when in reality virtually everything in most research

59

labs is either clear or some shade of yellow. I can count on one hand the number of organic chemicals that are bright blue or green. The chemicals are invariably in glassware jammed together backward and sideways, in what the set designer thought was a neat-looking combination. See the Nicholson-Karloff quickie *The Terror*, where in the witch's room we see a modern ground-glass three-neck flask, with the logo of the glass company clearly visible on its side. This during the Napoleonic wars.

DEREK LOWE, *Scotch Plains, N.J.*

Law of Economy of Characters. Movie budgets make it impossible for any film to contain unnecessary characters. Therefore, all characters in a movie are necessary to the story—even those who do not seem to be. Sophisticated viewers can use this law to deduce the identity of a person being kept secret by the movie's plot: This "mystery" person is always the only character in the movie who seems otherwise extraneous. (Cf. the friendly neighbor in *The Lady in White*; see also Unmotivated Close-up.)

Law of Economy of Instruction. Nobody is ever taught anything in a movie that they are not later called upon to use.

Law of Inevitable Immersion. Whenever characters are near a body of water, the chances are great that one of them will jump, fall, or be pushed into it. If this does occur, it is inevitable that the other character(s) will also jump, fall, or be pushed in.

Law of Inevitable Immersion

See *Sullivan's Travels* (swimming pool), *La Dolce Vita* (Roman fountain), *Tom Jones* (pond), *A Room with a View* (rural stream), *Summertime* (Grand Canal), etc.

STUART CLELAND, Chicago

Law of Inverse Wariness. The more dangerous the prisoner, the more lax the security precautions.

JEFF LEVIN, Rochester, N.Y.

Law of Movie Brand Loyalty. Thanks to product placement, all characters in a movie, no matter how heterogeneous or geographically dispersed, drink one brand of beer, use one brand of sporting equipment, drive cars produced by one company, etc.

PAUL A. LEE, Germantown, Wis.

Law of Take-out Chinese Food. Take-out Chinese food is eaten in one of only two situations: Communally by a large, multi-ethnic group enthusiastically working on a common project (*Reversal of Fortune*), or in bed by two post-coital lovers (*Annie Hall*). In the former case, the meal predicts success; in the latter, that the couple will break up.

PHILLIP L. GIANOS, Fullerton, Calif.

Law of Video Box Caricature, The. If you're trying to pick out a video and the actors on the box are cartooned caricatures which are not recognizable, pick another movie.

MARK BREWER, Lake Zurich, Ill.

Law of Vinyl Vulnerability. Unwritten rule in older Hollywood movies which decrees that any LP "vinyl" record album shown playing on a turntable must either be roughly grabbed and smashed to bits by a sad, depressed, or angry character who hates the song, or the tone arm needle must be violently dragged across its surface, thus ruining the record, in order to instantly hush a loud, annoying, and insensitive party crowd—whereupon the sad, depressed, or angry character demands in a loud voice that everybody must leave now.

ROBERT E. HUNT, JR.

Lawyer with One Case Scenario. In nearly all legal dramas, the lawyers involved have only one case—the case that the movie is about. They are never distracted by other cases, clients, or causes.

MARTIN J. KEENAN, ESQ., *Great Bend, Kans.*

Lenny Rule. Named for the gentle giant in Steinbeck's *Of Mice and Men*, this rule dictates that if a film character is of less than normal intelligence or ability, he or she will inadvertently get into serious trouble during the film.

STUART CLELAND, *Chicago*

Let Your Fingers Do the Driving. In any movie where the hero knows that other characters are in trouble, say because a time bomb is about to go off, he must jump into a car and drive like a lunatic across town to save them. No hero ever has a quarter for the pay phone.

BILL BECWAR, *Wauwatosa, Wis.*

Light Fantasic, The. Curious set design principle that requires malfunctioning computer equipment to be accompanied by purposeless, flashing light displays.

PAUL A. LEE, *Germantown, Wis.*

Lightning-Thunder-Downpour. In most suburban and rural thrillers involving a vulnerable heroine, a bolt of lightning, then thunder, and then an instantaneous downpour of hard rainfall occurs in rapid sequence, with no rumblings or darkened skies as forewarning. (The Wet Road Rule inevitably applies here.)

STEVE W. ZACK

Limo Exclusion Law. In any scene involving a limousine, where one actor is in the backseat talking to another actor outside the car, the scene will end with the actor in the car raising the window, reflecting back onto the outside actor the world he's stuck in.

MARK ORISTANO

Little Man Big Man Rule. Whenever one character is tall and the other is short and plump, the short one is always the brains and the tall one is the dummy (*Home Alone*, etc.).

DAVID ORMESHER, *Lakeland, Fla.*

Long-Haired Woman Seen from Behind. When approached by hero, inevitably turns out to be a man.

Love Boat Rule. Any character who coughs at any time has a terminal illness. Happens all the time on "The Love Boat," oddly enough.

JAMES R. JOKERST, Maryland

Mabel, the AT&T Phone. The AT&T telephones used in the movies are like standard models, except that the AT&T logo (known to company insiders as the Death Star) is printed on the heel of the handset, so that when an actor is speaking on the phone, it is clearly visible. AT&T makes no phones like this in real life. For numerous Mabel sightings, see *The Fugitive*. Mabel is never used in scenes calling for someone to be bashed to death with a telephone.

RICH ELIAS, Delaware, Ohio

Ma Bell Rule. Whenever a telephone is seen in a movie, the telephone will eventually ring.

KEN COX, Florence, S.C.

MacGuffin. Alfred Hitchcock's term for a plot element that "must seem to be of vital importance to the characters," even though its specific identify is immaterial. "It's the device, the gimmick, if you will, or the papers the spies are after," Hitchcock explained to François Truffaut in their book-length interview. Hitchcock illustrated with the story of two hunters in the Scottish Highlands. One asks the other what is in his package. "A MacGuffin," the other responds. "What's a MacGuffin?" "It's an apparatus for trapping lions." "But there

65

are no lions in the Highlands." "Then that's not a MacGuffin!" (See also, O'Guffin.)

MacLaine's Law of Female Fatality. If a movie features three female leads, one of them will die during childbirth. If there are five or more female leads, an additional female character will contract a terminal disease.

ANDY IHNATKO, *Westwood, Mass.*

Mad Dash into Traffic Rule. A car will always brake close enough for the running hero to touch it, and then dash into the next lane where the same thing happens with a car traveling in the opposite direction.

BARAK AND ELIZABETH MOORE, *Jerusalem, Israel*

Mad Slasher Movies. Movies starring a mad-dog killer who runs amok, slashing all of the other characters. The killer is frequently masked (as in *Halloween* and *Friday the 13th*), not because a serious actor would be ashamed to be seen in the role, but because then no actor at all is required; the only skills necessary are the ability to wear a mask and wield a machete. For additional reading, see *Splatter Movies*, by John ("Mutilation is the Message") McCarty.

Making that Last Sale. In the case of any impending disaster, natural or manmade, politicians will always arrive at the same conclusion: It is less important to issue a warning than to "avoid panicking the population." The reasoning is always the same: A warning will be bad for business.

EUGENE ACCARDO, *Brooklyn*

Mandatory Latrine Scene. In movies since 1980 with office settings, all major decisions are made by men of power while standing next to urinals and washbasins in the men's restroom.

DONNA MARTIN, *Kansas City*

Marathon Hero, The. A hero in pursuit of a purse-snatcher or getaway car can run for many blocks, even up the hills of San Francisco, without getting winded.

Martini Shot. In a production schedule, the last shot of principal photography at the end of the day is called the "Martini Shot," after which the crew can retire for the day and, in theory, enjoy a martini.

SAM HUMPHRIES

Meet Cute. Time-honored Hollywood method of having two important characters meet each other. In the Golden Age, it often involved the heroine exiting from a department store and dropping her packages after being bumped into by the hero. As they stoop to pick them up, their heads bump, leading to conversation, etc. In modern movies, Meet Cutes can be more ingenious. In *With Honors*, for example, a Harvard student meets a homeless man after a thesis falls through a sidewalk grating.

Mid-Wife Crisis. Any character whose wife and/or kids are introduced more than an

67

hour into the movie and who hugs and kisses any or all of them will be dead within the next twenty minutes. (E.g., "Goose" in *Top Gun*.)

EDWARD SAVIO, *San Francisco*

Milli-Vanilli Props. Novelty gadgets available today, but used in sci-fi/fantasy movies as futuristic devices. For example, in *Star Trek III: The Search For Spock*, McCoy is in a *Star Wars*–type bar with lava lamps.

TERRY FOX

Miracle of Available Parking Space. When a character needs a parking space, even on the busiest streets in the busiest cities, one is quickly found. For example, in *Lost in America*, Albert Brooks finds space for a Winnebago directly in front of an office building at midday in New York City. Corollary: When a character needs to pull into traffic, there is always a break.

PHILLIP L. GIANOS, *Fullerton, Calif.*

Miracle Twenty-five-pound Newborn Syndrome. Newborn babies in movies instantly look about seven months old, and weigh about twenty-five pounds. Their postpartum mother seems perfectly refreshed, made-up, and comfortable despite the gargantuan child she's just given birth to.

BARAK AND ELIZABETH MOORE, *Jerusalem, Israel*

Miraculous Projection Phenomenon. Ability of apparently normal computer, TV, and movie screens to project their images onto

Milli-Vanilli Props

the face of an actor. In extreme cases, the audience is able the read the crisply focused words from a computer screen directly off an actor's face.

RICHARD ROHRDANZ, *West Kennebunk, Maine*

Mirror Gimmick. Tired old cinemagraphic trick in which we think we are seeing a character, but then the camera pans and we realize we were only looking in a mirror.

ARDEN J. COOPER, *Warren, Mich.*

Mirror Gimmick II. We see the hero in serious conversation (trying to propose marriage, for example). After a few lines the camera pans back and we realize he was only rehearsing his speech. (See *Forever Young.*)

LAUREL VAN DYKE, *Kokomo, Ind.*

Mission Control Syndrome. Tired but insidious device in which filmmaker prompts the audience to react after failing to explain why anyone should care. The action is intercut with footage of a contrived surrogate audience, reacting with mounting tension—and then ecstatic, arm-waving, paper-hurling jubilation. Easy in sports movies; over-labored in films like *WarGames* (spurious Pentagon war room), *The Right Stuff* (mission control), all the *Airport* movies (control tower), *The Hunt for Red October* (Pentagon again). Most end-of-the-world movies have an obligatory roomful of scientists to monitor approaching doom.

ANGUS MCCALLUM, *New York City*

"Mr. Electricity Is Our Friend" Principle.
The safety fence around a transformer or
similar high-voltage equipment magically
becomes charged when a bad guy is thrown
against it, invariably with spectacular re-
sults. When the good guy hits the same
fence earlier in the fight, nothing happens.

ERIC AMICK, *Columbia, Md.*

Mr. Magooser Interface. Computers in
movies are often unable to display anything
more than three lines of very large letters
during normal operations. All the computers in the Star Trek films, for instance,
sport the classic Magooser Interface; during
a crisis, all screens clear themselves of useful information and display RED ALERT in
jumbo letters, instead of informing the
crew what exactly the problem is and how
they might solve it.

ANDY IHNATKO, *Westwood, Mass.*

Moe Rule of Bomb Disposal. Used by bomb
squad experts in movies. When they know
that cutting one wire will deactivate the
bomb and cutting the other will make it
explode, the correct wire to cut is always
"Moe." All movie bomb experts clamp
their cutters around one wire but end up
cutting the other at the last moment.
("Eenie, meenie, minie . . . snip!")

ANDY IHNATKO, *Westwood, Mass.*

Monk's Reward. A surprising final line or
image, tagged on after the credits have fin-
ished rolling (e.g., in *Airplane!*, the fellow
in the taxicab at the airport, still yakking).

71

So named because it usually takes monklike devotion to sit through the credits to get to it.

SERDOR YEGULALP

Movieland, CA, and Filmtown, N.Y. The two towns which are the setting for all movies in which characters dial the phony numbers (408) 555–XXXX and (212) 555–XXXX. Any phone call made to these exchanges will connect you to a fabulous movie celebrity or extra!

ANDY IHNATKO, *Westwood, Mass.*

Movie Medicine Men. No disease is incurable for the elderly doctors or medicine men of third-world cultures, who always produce a secret powder or herb. The medicine's action is triggered by the simple poetic philosophy which accompanies the treatment.

Murphy's Law. In movies made before 1985, any character named "Murphy" was a cop, a priest, a drunk, a tough guy, or all of the above. *Murphy's Romance* was the first to break with this rule. Prior to TV's Murphy Brown, all Murphys were male. Any character named Murphy will sooner or later be shown in a saloon, or drinking heavily.

ROBERT F. MURPHY, *Providence, R.I.*

Myopia Rule. Little girls who wear glasses in the movies always tell the truth. Little boys who wear glasses in the movies always lie.

GENE SISKEL

Myopic Visionary. In movies in which time travel or nostalgia takes us back to the 1940s or 1950s, the obligatory character who is loudly skeptical of the viability of television or Japanese industry announces he's about to go out and buy an Edsel.

ANDY IHNATKO, *Westwood, Mass.*

Mysterious Object Antecedents Myth. Whenever a movie involves time travel, there will always be an object that travels between the past and future without ever having actually come from anywhere. Example: in the beginning of *Somewhere in Time*, an old Jane Seymour gives the young Christopher Reeve a pocket watch. He travels back in time to find her, taking the watch with him, and accidentally leaves it there. She keeps it, grows old, and—voilà—the cycle repeats itself. But where did the pocket watch come from in the first place?

BARBARA KELSEY

Mystery Guest. At a crowded table, the sole empty chair and place setting, positioned right between the camera and the actors. Traditionally placed there in memory of L.B. Mayer, whose second coming was foretold by the prophet Winchell.

ANDY IHNATKO, *Westwood, Mass.*

Mystery of the Levitating Ghost. If the hero can jump through the wall of the moving subway train, why doesn't he fall through the floor?

BILL BECWAR, *Wauwatosa, Wis.*

Myth of the Seemingly Ordinary Day.
The day begins like any other, with a man
getting up, having breakfast, reading the
paper, leaving the house, etc. His activities
are so uneventful they are boring. That is
the tip-off. No genuine ordinary day can
be allowed to be boring in a movie. Only
seemingly ordinary days—which inevitably
lead up to a shocking scene of violence,
which punctuates the seeming ordinariness.

Nah Reflex. Character sees someone but
can't believe his eyes, so shakes his head
and says "Nah." Inevitably it is the person
it couldn't be.

JOHN WECKMUELLER, *Menomonie, Wis.*

Nazi Sentry Syndrome. Nazi soldiers on
sentry duty invariably suffer from acute
drowsiness. Their peripheral vision shrinks
to the area directly in front of them, and
they become hard of hearing. When at-
tacked, their vocal chords can produce
only muffled Teutonic grunts.

DAVID NEVARD, *Waltham, Mass.*

Near Miss Kiss. The hero and heroine are
about to kiss. Their lips are a quarter of
an inch apart—but then they're interrupted.

DOUGLAS W. TOPHAM, *Woodland Hills, Calif.*

Neon Sign Rule. Whenever the leading
male is hiding out or thrown out of his
house by his wife and has to spend the
night in a sleazy hotel, he always gets the
room with the hotel's blinking neon sign
right outside his window.

EUGENE ACCARDO, *Brooklyn*

Nerd Rule. In any teenager movie the nerd character will, by the end of the film, be dating the prettiest girl in the school, proving that nerds are people, too.

LISA MARTIN, Toronto

Newton Improved, or, the Nine Laws of Cartoon Thermodynamics. (1). Any body suspended in space will remain in space until made aware of its situation. Daffy Duck steps off a cliff, expecting further pastureland. He loiters in midair, soliloquizing flippantly, until he chances to look down. At this point, the familiar principle of thirty-two feet per second per second takes over. (2). Any body in motion will tend to remain in motion until solid matter intervenes suddenly. Whether shot from a cannon or in hot pursuit on foot, cartoon characters are so absolute in their momentum that only a telephone pole or an outsize boulder retards their forward motion absolutely. Sir Isaac Newton called this sudden termination of motion the stooge's surcease. (3). Any body passing through solid matter will leave a perforation conforming to its perimeter. Also called the silhouette of passage, this phenomenon is the specialty of victims of directed-pressure explosions and of reckless cowards who are so eager to escape that they exit directly through the wall of a house, leaving a cookie-cutout-perfect hole. The threat of skunks or matrimony often catalyzes this reaction. (4). The time required for an object to fall twenty stories is greater than or equal to the time it takes for whoever knocked it off the ledge to spiral down twenty flights to attempt to capture it unbroken. Such an object is inevitably priceless, the attempt to capture it inevitably unsuccessful. (5). All principles of gravity are negated by fear. Psychic forces are sufficient in most bodies for a shock to propel them directly away from the earth's surface. A spooky noise or an adversary's signature sound will induce motion upward, usually to the cradle of a chandelier, a treetop, or the crest of a flag-pole. The feet of a character who is running or the wheels of a speeding auto need never touch the ground, especially when in flight. (6). As speed increases, objects can be in several places at once. This is particularly true of tooth-and-claw fights, in which a character's head may be glimpsed emerging from the cloud of altercation at several places simultaneously. This effect is common as well among bodies that are spinning or being throttled. A "wacky" character has the option of self-replication only at manic high speeds and may ricochet off walls to achieve the velocity required. (7.) Certain bodies can pass through solid walls painted to resemble tunnel entrances; others cannot. This trompe l'oeil inconsistency has baffled generations, but at least it is known that whoever paints an entrance on a wall's surface to trick an opponent will be unable to pursue him into this theoretical space. The painter is flattened against the wall when he attempts to follow into the painting. This is ultimately a problem of art, not of science. (8). Any violent rearrangement of feline matter is impermanent. Cartoon cats possess even more deaths than the traditional nine lives might comfortably afford. They can be decimated, spliced, splayed, accordion-pleated, spindled, or disassembled, but they cannot be destroyed. After a few moments of blinking self pity, they reinflate, elongate, snap back, or solidify. Corollary: A cat will assume the shape of its container. (9). For every vengeance there is an equal and opposite revengeance. This is the one law of animated cartoon motion that also applies to the physical world at large. For that reason, we need the relief of watching it happen to a duck instead.

MARK O'DONNELL, *New York*

Newton's Laws Repealed. In which action becomes mysteriously decoupled from reaction, usually in connection with a firearm. Typically, a bullet from the hero's handgun lifts the villain off his feet and hurls him backward (often through one of those ubiquitous plate glass windows that cars like to drive through) while the hero doesn't budge a millimeter. (Action equals reaction, right? The hero should be hurled backward with equal force.)

ROBERT J. LANG, *Altadena, Calif.*

Nightmare Reflex. Character wakes from a nightmare by sitting bolt upright in a bed with bulging eyes and sweat all over his face.

FRASER SMITH, *Tampa*

Nineteen RMS W/VU. Unless the point is to establish poverty, the apartments occupied by movie characters always look much larger and more expensive than anyone on their salary could afford. If the point is to establish "colorful" poverty, the occupants are so poor they can only afford to furnish with antiques.

Noble Savage Syndrome. Thrown into the company of a native tribe of any description, the protagonist discovers the true meaning of life and sees through the sham of modern civilization. Wisdom and sensitivity are inevitably possessed by any race, class, age group, or ethnic or religious minority that has been misunderstood. Such movies seem well intentioned at first glance, but replace one stereotype for another; the natives seem noble, but never real. They may be starving, but if they're noble and have a few good songs, why worry?

ROBERT F. MURPHY

No-Fail Pregnancy Predictor. Any woman of childbearing age in any movie who is ever nauseous.

BARAK AND ELIZABETH MOORE, *Jerusalem, Israel*

Non-Answering Pet. In any horror or suspense movie, if the family pet does not come after being called at least twice by the protagonist or a member of his family, he is dead. This sometimes happens after he has served as an example of the Law of Canine/Feline Superperception (q.v.).

JOHN SHANNON

O'Guffin. Inspired by Hitchcock's Mac-Guffin (q.v.). A scene or sequence that has nothing to do with the plot of the film. Usually found lurking in B-movies, as an entertainment filler device, to mask the fact that the film has little or no actual story. See the Compulsory Topless Bar Scene in most R-rated cop action movies.

JIM AND ROSE PFEIFER, *Southfield, Mich.*

Odd Couple Formula. Seemingly incompatible characters are linked to each other in a plot which depends on their differences for its comic and dramatic interest (c.f. *Tango and Cash, Homer and Eddie, Lethal Weapon, Loose Cannons*). Essential that one member of each team be a slob, as revealed by presence of fast-food wrappers in backseat of his Hollywood Cop Car (q.v.).

Odd Information Clue. Bad exposition is often a giveaway to plot points, since there must be a reason why we're getting all this otherwise inexplicable information. The most trivial fact delivered in the most off-hand manner in Act I will prove monumentally significant, come denouement time.

JEFF LEVIN, *Rochester, N.Y.*

Odds on Edge Rule. The odds that a car in real life will be able to travel any appreciable distance balanced on two wheels: 1 in 7 million. The odds that this will happen during a chase scene in a movie: 1 in 43.

One Punch Fallacy. The myth that any movie hero can knock out any villain with a solid right to the jaw. (In any collision between a human skull and an unprotected human

79

hand, the hand will be the worse for the experience.)

ANTHONY BRUCE GILPIN, *Riverside, Calif.*

One-at-a-Time Attack Rule. In any situation where the hero is alone, surrounded by dozens of bad guys, they will always obligingly attack one at a time. (See any Schwarzenegger movie.)

BARBARA KELSEY

One Size Fits All (1). Any stolen clothing or shoes will perfectly fit any male character whether they were stolen from a clothesline or removed from a Nazi guard, police officer, lookout, etc., who was overpowered and whose identity the clothing thief has now assumed.

DONA KIGHT, *Chicago*

One Size Fits All (2). If a woman character steals clothing to disguise herself, the clothing, if male, will be too big. If female, it will be much too skimpy and revealing.

Oops, Sorry! Rule. Character sees person from behind on street, thinks it is someone he knows, runs up and confronts person, inevitably to discover it is someone else.

DAN SAUNDERS, *Oakland, Calif.*

Oscilloscope Fantastic. Test instruments are used to display Lissajous figures, sine waves, or other meaningless curves and lines to suggest that something mysteriously technical is happening in the laboratory.

CHARLES PEKLENK

Paint and Sufferink. Scenes in a G-rated animated feature which would have guaranteed the film at least a PG if it had been shot in live-action.

ANDY IHNATKO, *Westwood, Mass.*

Parent/Child Polarity Predictor. If the parents are good the kids will be bad, or vice versa, unless they get along, in which case they're either both good or both bad.

STEVE WIDEMAN

Pass Bypass Principle. Any theater that accepts passes will invariably exclude their use for any movie worth seeing.

MIKE SILVERMAN, *Holliston, Mass.*

Penguin Error. Bad guy keeps good guy alive to witness the great evil he will commit, allowing good guy to prevent it. See *Under Siege,* where the evil genius played by Tommy Lee Jones makes the fatal mistake of keeping Steven Seagal alive to witness the destruction of Honolulu. Named for the Penguin and all the other Batman enemies, who made this error weekly in the old series. (See also Fallacy of the Talking Killer.)

JOSEPH HOLMES

Perfectly Alternated Vehicle Rule. During all car chases through traffic, all of the vehicles not directly involved in the chase are arranged so that the chase vehicles can weave left and right continuously, as in a "Road and Track" handling test.

TOM RATCLIFFE, *Toronto*

Perk Girl. Used as an emblem of the hero's power. Appears in early scene, usually unclothed, with fashionable body. We usually do not see her face. She has no dialogue. She walks across the frame, a possession he takes for granted. Even though it seems from the context that they have an easy intimacy, we never see her again in the movie, nor is she is ever referred to. (See opening of *Wall Street*.)

MICHAEL E. ISBELL

Phantom Karaoke Machine. Unseen electronic prompter which explains how a small group of people who spontaneously take to a stage happen to know an entire number by heart, including harmonies and stage choreography. . . . Especially useful when the performers come from an era which precedes the song by decades.

ANDY IHNATKO, *Westwood, Mass.*

Phantom Phantom Rule. In any case where a movie crew member or unauthorized person accidentally appears in the background of a shot, a legend will develop to explain the appearance—usually involving suicide, a shotgun, and the spirit of the deceased haunting the set. Examples: the folklore surrounding *The Wizard of Oz* and *Three Men and a Baby*.

COLIN M. CHISHOLM

Plot Pointer. Character who appears, delivers no more than a half-dozen lines of dialogue crucial to the plot, and then disappears for good. Plot Pointers are raised and

Phantom Karoake Machine

trained exclusively for the movie industry on a free-range farm in Vermont, and descend from a breeding pair originally developed in 1932 for MGM musicals.

ANDY IHNATKO, Westwood, Mass.

Pointy Object Principle. If the bad guy attacks the good guy with a sharp object during a fight and it gets embedded in the wall or floor, the bad guy will be killed by it, generally by falling on it.

ERIC AMICK, Columbia, Md.

Poisoned Phone Booth. Any time the hero, on the run, stops at a phone booth to call for help, he inevitably reaches the person trying to kill him. The villain tells the hero to stay right there, then sends killers to finish him off. The hero wanders away and an unsuspecting extra enters the phone booth, where *he's* the one machine-gunned instead. Cut to: the hero, the horrified look on his face showing us he now understands The Full Extent Of The Conspiracy.

DAVID DANIEL, Smyrna, Ga.

Police Escort Pause. Two police officers taking away an apprehended criminal will always pause as they pass the protagonist in order to allow the criminal to say something really nasty, vow revenge, or perhaps just spit.

JOSEPH HOLMES

Polite Killer Rule. It is a rule of horror etiquette that a monster must wait—all night if necessary—by a window in the intended victim's home until such time as he is effectively invited in by said victim opening a curtain and looking out of this window. Then and only then does the glass become breakable, and the monster or mad slasher is able to crash through and attack the intended target. This is an extension of the child's Monster under the Bed Rule (monsters under the bed cannot pull you off the bed unless you dangle a limb over the edge).

FRANK P. SCALFANO

Poor Phone Manners. No one ever says "good-bye" when talking on the phone in the movies. The conversation ends, according to the script, and the character just hangs up the phone.

DAWSON E. RAMBO, Pelham Manor, N.Y.

Pops Principle, The. In movies with teenage characters, there is usually a character named Pops who runs the local hangout or dance club.

DONALD MUNSCH, Sherman, Tex.

PO Rule. No matter how many car chases, action set pieces, shoot-outs, or explosions have occurred, the villain is never really ready to be captured or killed until the hero picks himself up, dusts the broken glass off, sniffs the cordite in the air, and says, "Now he's *really* beginning to piss me off!"

DAWSON E. RAMBO, Pelham Manor, N.Y.

Possessed Golf Cart. Any layperson who gets behind the wheel of a golf cart will eventually drive the vehicle into the nearest body of water. (Cf. *Legal Eagles*, *Stakeout*, etc.)

DAN GUTOWSKY, *Lansing, Mich.*

Possible Implausible Rule. Movie audiences are quicker to accept the impossible than the implausible.

DAVID BURD, *East Stroudsburg, Pa.*

Premature Disarmament. Movie heroes have a habit of optimistically tossing away their weapons too soon. This act is usually preceded by the Instant Diagnosis Syndrome, where the hero, after a first strike/punch/hit, wrongly decides after a cursory glance that the bad guy is unconscious, dead, or disabled.

HARRISON CHEUNG

Prematurely Lightened Loads (aka, the "Leave It, It's Too Heavy and Besides it Might Save My Life" Syndrome). Situations where the good guy disables the first of many bad guys and when given the choice to take the bad guy's guns and ammo, doesn't do so. Also applies to water, radios, flare guns, car keys, maps, and the like.

ERIC M. DAVITT, *Toronto*

Principle of Evil Marksmanship. The bad guys are always lousy shots in the movies. Three villains with Uzis will go after the hero, spraying thousands of rounds which miss him, after which he picks them off with a handgun.

JIM MURPHY, *New York City*

Principle of Inverse Critical Plausibility. The proven inverse relationship between the quality of a film and the number of rave reviews in its ads which originated from publications and TV shows with the word "Hollywood" in their titles.

ANDY IHNATKO, *Westwood, Mass.*

Principle of Pedestrian Pathology. Whenever a character on foot is being pursued by one in a car, the pedestrian inevitably makes the mistake of running down the middle of the street, instead of ducking down a narrow alley, into a building, behind a telephone pole, etc. All that saves such pedestrians is the fact that in such scenes the character on foot can always outrun the car.

STUART CLELAND, *Chicago*

Principle of Selective Lethality. The lethality of a weapon varies, depending on the situation. A single arrow will drop a stampeding bison in its tracks, but it takes five or six to kill an important character. A single bullet will always kill an extra on the spot, but it takes dozens to bring down the hero.

BARRY ZIMMERMAN

Prop Recycling. Sci-fi/fantasy movies sometimes borrow futuristic devices from each other because of low budgets. Example: The ghost detectors in *Ghostbusters II* became motion detectors in *They Live*.

TERRY FOX

Psychic Flip. Amazing ability of any actor or actress to open a book to within five pages of the one they are looking for. If the proper page is not found on the first try, it will take no more than three flips to find it.

KYLE SIPPLES

Psychic Partner. In countless cop movies: (1). Hero comes in the door of his apartment/house to a ringing phone. (2). Answering it, he hears his partner say something like, "You'd better turn on channel 3 *right now*! (3). The hero does so, only to see a news report *just beginning* that brings a crucial development or clue to the plot. Since the news report is just beginning, how did the partner know about it?

DAWSON E. RAMBO, *Pelham Manor, N.Y.*

Push! Push! Scene. Obligatory natural childbirth scene, which is to boomer movies what the chase is in a Dirty Harry picture. Modern version of the old "boil water, hot water, and lots of it!" scene.

Quick Recovery Syndrome. Any person critical to the movie's sequel (such as the hero's buddy) can be on the edge of death throughout the film, but by the end of the movie recovers fully. See *Beverly Hills Cop II*, where Ronny Cox is shot in the heart at point-blank range but is ready to leave the hospital within seventy-two hours, or *Licence to Kill*, where Bond's newlywed buddy loses the lower half of his body to a shark, but is joking at the film's end.

TED MILLER, *Green Bay, Wis.*

Radar Bullet Phenomenon. A mysterious force which ensures that if a bullet does not hit a major character in an instantly lethal place (i.e., the head or heart), it won't hit any bones or vital organs, and will rarely do serious damage. In the truck chase in *Raiders of the Lost Ark*, for example, Indy is shot in the upper arm, from the side. The bullet doesn't break his arm, though from that angle it should, and he retains full use of his arm. Near the end of *RoboCop*, the bad guy shoots Murphy's partner Lewis half a dozen times with a large-caliber pistol, but she's still able to crawl twenty or thirty feet, and then lift, aim, and fire a huge rifle.

JON WOOLF, *Beavercreek, Ohio*

Rain as Emotion Syndrome. When an actor is unable to register shock, the director calls for rain and instructs the actor to make no attempt to avoid getting wet.

NIGEL SEARLE, *Venice, Fla.*

Rattlesnake Rectal Regulation. In any comedy set in the Old West, if a character lowers his pants to move his bowels, he will be horrified to find he has chosen a secluded spot that is home to a rattlesnake. (See *City Slickers II* and *Lightning Jack*.)

Reverse Doppler Effect. Phenomenon only found in movies where an incoming artillery shell is heard decreasing in pitch. I was quite surprised in Vietnam when, during the course of a mortar attack, the shells were heard to increase in pitch, as any physics student could have predicted.

JOHN D. MCCLUSKEY

Reynolds Ramp. Heavy steel sewer pipes, railroad ties, or piles of dirt left in the road which cause cars to jump, flip, and/or barrel-roll in spectacular slow-motion fashion when they pass over them. N.B.: Force of attraction between a car and a Reynolds Ramp increases geometrically with the value, age, and scarcity of the car in question. No car driven by Burt Reynolds can avoid one.

ANDY IHNATKO, *Westwood, Mass.*

Rising Sidewalk. No female character in an action film can flee more than fifty feet before falling flat on her face. Someone then has to go back and help her up, while the monster/villain/enemy gains ground.

JAMES PORTANOVA, *Fresh Meadows, N.Y.*

Rock Candy Postulate. No hero is ever cut by glass while leaping through windows.

DANIEL ALVARADO, *Arleta, Calif.*

Rock 'n' Roll Lite Rule. Whenever a fictitious rock star sings or plays, the music will be wildly cheered by thousands of screaming fans, even though it isn't fit for a K mart opening.

SAM WAAS, *Houston*

Rule of Chronic Tunnel Vision. In a horror movie, the character being stalked has vision limited to the camera's field of view.

Rock 'n' Roll Lite Rule

Therefore, anyone coming at any angle not directly ahead will invariably scare the living daylights out of him or her.

DANIEL ALVARADO, *Arleta, Calif.*

Rule of Reverse Explosive Proportionality. The quality of a movie containing an explosion is in roughly reverse proportion to the number of times that same explosion is shown from different angles. Example: The exploding van is shown four times in the movie *Dead Heat*, earning it a one-star rating.

MARTIN VASKO, *San Francisco*

Rule of the Hallucinogenic Carousel. Any time the hero or heroine is being pursued and the chase leads to a merry-go-round, the villain will be unable to catch his prey. Rather than wait ten seconds for the carousel to complete a revolution, the villain will immediately hop on in hot pursuit. During the chase the audience is often treated to weird calliope music. No real carousel uses such music; it sounds as if the sound track was switched with the fun house.

JOHN E. ROCHE, *San Francisco*

Rule of the Purloined Letter. When a character's mail has been regularly intercepted, all letters will be carefully preserved by the interceptor. There will be a heart-touching scene at the end where the character finally gets all of those letters and reads them one by one.

ANDY IHNATKO, *Westwood, Mass.*

Rule of the Purloined Letter

Saliva Syndrome. Heroines who are tied up have an uncanny compulsion to spit in the villain's face. In response, the villain inevitably smiles.

Satin Static Cling Phenomenon. The heroine, after spending the night cavorting with a man she met only a few hours earlier, carefully pulls up the bedsheet to modestly cover herself when he says good-bye the next morning. Amazingly, the sheets stay in place even while she is sitting up. This rule does not apply in movies in which Madonna or Sharon Stone appear.

ALAN JOHNSON, *Phoenix*

Scary Old Man (or Woman). Used in horror movies to warn the young people to stay away from the old house, castle, woods, etc. Usually portrayed as a homeless person or someone that all the townspeople regard as crazy. (See *Friday the 13th* movies.)

EUGENE ACCARDO, *Brooklyn*

Sci-Fi Currency Conversion. In any science fiction movie, anywhere in the galaxy, currency is refered to as "credits."

SAM HUMPHRIES

Sean Connery Exception. Bald men are not allowed to perform romantic kissing in the movies unless they are later revealed to be villains, or are Sean Connery.

Seeing-Eye Man. Function performed by most men in Hollywood feature films. Involves a series of shots in which (1) the man sees something, (2) he points it out to the woman, (3) she then sees it too, often nodding in agreement, gratitude, amusement, or relief.

First identified by LINDA WILLIAMS.

"See You Next Wednesday." This line was used in the telephone call from space in Stanley Kubrick's *2001*, and has since been used in every single film directed by John Landis. For that matter, Kubrick has had a scene involving a bathroom in every one of *his* films.

Semi-Obligatory Lyrical Interlude (Semi-OLI). Scene in which soft focus and slow motion are used while a would-be hit song is performed on the sound track and the lovers run through a pastoral setting. Common from the mid-1960s to the mid-1970s; replaced in 1980s with the Semi-Obligatory Music Video (q.v.).

Semi-Obligatory Music Video (Semi-OMV). Three-minute sequence within otherwise ordinary narrative structure, in which a song is played at top volume while movie characters experience spasms of hyperkinetic behavior and stick their faces into the camera lens. If a band is seen, the Semi-OMV is inevitably distinguished by the director's inability to find a fresh cinematic approach to the challenge of filming a slack-jawed drummer.

Sequel. A filmed deal.

Seven Minute Rule. In the age of the seven-minute attention span (inspired by the average length between TV commercials), action movies aimed at teenagers are constructed out of several seven-minute segments. At the end of each segment, another teenager is dead. When all the teenagers are dead (or, if you arrived in the middle, when the same dead teenager turns up twice), the movie is over.

Sex-Specific Disintegrating Outfit. When the male and female characters in a trashy action movie go to hell and back, only the woman's clothing begins to disintegrate.

DAVE POLSKY, *Ottawa, Canada*

Shelley Winters Index. In scenes where a character must hold his or her breath and swim underwater, the elapsed time in seconds between the "pfoooahh!" of the last audience member giving up trying to match the time, and the character's finally reaching a supply of air. For instance, in *The Abyss*, Ed Harris's SWI is 3.2; in *Star Trek IV* William Shatner's is 40.0; and in *The Poseidon Adventure* Shelley Winters herself racks up an impressive SWI of 149.9.

ANDY IHNATKO, *Westwood, Mass.*

Short Life Syndrome. Night watchmen in horror movies have a life expectancy of twelve seconds.

SAM WAAS, *Houston*

Short Time Syndrome. Applies to prison, war, or police movies, where the hero only has a few more days until he is free, his

Shelley Winters Index

tour is over, or he can retire with full pension. Whenever such a character makes the mistake of mentioning his remaining time ("Three days and I'm outta here!") he will die before the end of that time.

Simultaneous Recovery Syndrome. When a group of movie characters is rendered unconscious, all characters awake at approximately the same time.

> JEFF BRAUN, *Seattle*, and
> BILL RUSSELL, *Richmond, Ind.*

Sinatra's Law. In any Odd Couple Formula movie, the buddies will run into a situation in which the normal partner is unable to function successfully. The other partner, representing the eccentric, abnormal, and supposedly wrong way of doing things, will invariably say, "Let's try doing it . . . my way." (See Eddie Murphy in *48 HRS*, Mel Gibson in *Lethal Weapon,* etc.)

> PATRICK DORSEY, *Huntington, N.Y.*

Sinister Stretch Limo Rule. Movie villians are often chauffeured in black stretch limos with darkly tinted windows. This does not make them an object of curiosity in the rundown warehouse districts or dangerous inner city streets where they usually are found. (See also "Limo Exclusion Law.")

Siskel's Saw. "It's amazing how many movies are not as interesting as a documentary of the same actors sitting around talking over lunch."

> GENE SISKEL

Siskel's Theory of Relativity. The movie is moving slowly when you begin to look at your watch. It is moving very slowly when you begin to tap your watch to be sure it hasn't stopped.

GENE SISKEL

Slide Show Rule. During briefings about the search for a sinister international criminal, the chief good guy will hold a magic lantern show, projecting a blurry picture of the bad guy and intoning, "He's a former member of the KGB/IRA/Red Brigade." (Cf. *Nighthawks, In the Line of Fire*)

CHRIS FISANICK, *Barnesboro, Penn.*

Sound Track Surprise. Occurs when the audience members think the song they are hearing is just part of the sound track and not being heard by the characters, but it suddenly ends when a character turns off the stereo or radio.

KYLE L. CAIN, *Sugar Land, Tex.*

Stalled Truck Technique. Whenever a cop is chasing quarry in an alley, a truck will back into the alley, cutting off the cop. The truck then mysteriously becomes rooted to the spot, and the cop jumps out of the car. Cut to: the quarry getting away. Cut back to: the cop pounding the roof of his car. (In rural movies, substitute narrow dirt road for alley, and farm tractor for truck. See also "Camel, Slow-Moving.")

MICHAEL J. PILLING, *Maple Ridge, B.C., Canada*

Stanton-Walsh Rule. No movie featuring either Harry Dean Stanton or M. Emmet Walsh in a supporting role can be altogether bad. Exceptions are *Chattahoochee*, starring Walsh, and *Wild at Heart*, starring Stanton.*

Still Out There Somewhere. Obligatory phrase in Dead Teenager and Mad Slasher Movies, where it is triggered by the words, "The body was never found. They say he/she is . . ."

Stradivarius Rule. Whenever a violin is an important part of a movie plot, it is a Stradivarius. Whenever such an instrument does appear on the screen, it is, of course, doomed.

BOB GOODMAN, *New York University*

"Stranger in a Strange Land" Principle. When a star of a movie shows up in a new town, that person will be famous in that town by the end of the movie.

Street Furniture Rules. (1). All movies set prior to 1955 should have yellow and black stop signs. (2). All movies set prior to 1982 should lack *USA Today* boxes.

HANK OTTERY, *Chicago*

Stupid Adult Rule. In any situation where a child or teenager finds that the group is in danger, or has the solution to a problem that stumps all the adults, the adults will

---

*Matthew J. Carson of Wallingford, Pa. writes in to argue that Michael J. Pollard should be included in this rule, but Carson's defense of Pollard in *Tango and Cash* is less than convincing.)

invariably refuse to listen to the kid. This continues either until it's almost too late, or until the kid takes matters into his/her own hands. Especially likely in any episode of "Star Trek" where Wesley Crusher appears.

ANDREW COLES, Toronto

Sturgeon's Law. "Ninety percent of everything is crap." (First formulated in the 1950s by the science fiction author Theodore Sturgeon; quoted here because it so manifestly applies to motion pictures.)

Substandard Movie Tires. Movie characters have worn tires on their cars. Even an easy stop from five miles an hour produces a skidding sound as if the brakes were locked from thirty miles an hour. Comfortably rounding a corner causes tire squealing. Even the wimpiest of cars makes a brief burning-rubber sound as it gently accelerates from a stop.

JIM COLLIER, Dallas

Superfluous Pump. Dramatic effect in gun movies. The gunman has fired multiple shots and then when he has his victim cornered, unnecessarily pumps (cocks) his weapon, an action that would eject an unused shell.

J. FERGUSON, Elmhurst, Ill.

Surprise Gender Switch. In any competition where one of the opponents is wearing a garment that conceals body and face, if that opponent wins, in the next shot the head-covering is pulled off to reveal—gasp!—that the opponent was a woman!

Surround Sound Reciprocal Principle. The amount of surround sound track usage is inversely proportional to the amount of dialogue worth hearing.

DAVID KALIN, *San Francisco*

SWAT Movie. Sinks Without a Trace.

RICH ELIAS, *Delaware, Ohio*

Technopyromania. Affliction that compels filmmakers and special effects people to depict the malfunction of computers as being accompanied by smoke, flames, showers of pyrotechnic sparks, frenzied flashing lights, and wildly spinning tape drives spewing tape into the air.

PAUL A. LEE, *Germantown, Wis.*

Teetotaler Relapse Syndrome. Any character introduced as a recovering alcoholic who's been off the bottle for an extended period will go back to drinking sometime during the film. Examples: Michael Douglas in *Basic Instinct*, Kenneth Branagh in *Peter's Friends*.

JEFF LEVIN, *Rochester, N.Y.*

Telltale File Giveaway. Any time the good guy surreptitiously pilfers from a file cabinet, something will happen to force him to flee the scene shortly after discovering the needed secret information. His hasty departure will cause him to leave the file in a state that allows the bad guy to deduce who was there.

RICK NEWBY, *College Place, Wash.*

Ten Kickboxing Movies Still to Be Made: (1). *A Kickboxer Christmas*; (2). *Kalifornia*

Kickboxer; (3). *Where the Kickboxers Are*;
(4). *Kickboxing in Fruit*; (5). *Kickboxer
Karwash*; (6). *Oh to be Kickboxing*;
(7). *Nick: The Kickboxer Who Couldn't
Read*; (8). *So Many Kickboxers*; (9). *Jaws
VII: The Kickboxer*; (10). *Kickboxer VI,
Jaws II*.

ADAM PLANTINGA, *Grand Rapids, Mich.*, and
HADLEY BETH, *Urbana, Ill.*

Thanks, but No Thanks. When two people
have just had a heart-to-heart conversation,
as Person A starts to leave room, Person B
says (tentatively) "Bob?" A pauses, turns,
and says "Yes?" B says, "Thanks."

BETSEY BRUNK

Theory of Movie Relativity. If you watch
the credits to the very end you will see at
least one person listed who has the same
last name as the director or one of the producers.

DAVID BURD, *East Stroudsburg, Pa.*

There-Goes-the-Neighborhood Rule. In
horror movies, no matter how many ghostly
apparitions or psychokillers appear in a
house, the owners will not leave it. In fact,
the more scared they get, the more deter-
mined they are to stay put. Apparently
they're earning some kind of "scream
equity." (Cf. *Amityville Horror*, etc.)

RAPHAEL CARTER, *Tempe, Ariz.*

Third Hand. Invisible appendage used by
Rambo in *Rambo*, in the scene where he
hides from the enemy by completely plaster-
ing himself inside a mud bank. Since it is
impossible to cover yourself with mud with-

103

out at least one hand free to do the job, Rambo must have had a third, invisible, hand. This explains a lot about the movie.

Tic Reversi. Nervous disorder that causes an actor to repeatedly pick up and put down an item upon each cut between reverse shots in a scene.

PAUL A. LEE, *Germantown, Wis.*

Tijuana. In modern Horny Teenager Movies, performs the same symbolic function as California did for the beatniks, Marakech did for the hippies, and Paris did for the Lost Generation.

Timely Bladder Syndrome. When hero is one of a group of people, he goes off to the toilet or other secluded room just as the villains attack. Glimpsing the action from the bathroom, he is unknown to the bad guys and thus still free to respond. See *Die Hard* (back room), *Under Siege* (meat locker), *Passenger 57* (airplane toilet).

KEVIN WAN, *Seattle, Wash.*

Title Tease Warning. Movies that alternate long passages of plot with opening credits for lengthy periods of screen time reflect the attention span of their creators and should be avoided.

R.R. KUNZ

Traction Action Rule. Whenever there's a patient in traction with a cast on his leg and ropes attached to a pulley system, a visitor will inevitably cause the cast to go up into the air and the patient to experience severe pain.

RAUL H. MARQUEZ, *Maryland*

Traction Action Rule

Training Sequence. In any movie culminating in a competition, this is the montage during which the hero is turned from a loser into a winner through the inspired but merciless tutelage of the Coach Figure, who alternates between wisdom and sadism. See Pat Morita in *The Karate Kid*, Burgess Meredith in *Rocky*, John Candy in *Cool Runnings*, etc. The training inevitably includes one lesson that will be remembered in a flashback during a crucial moment of the competition, giving the hero fresh inspiration.

TRISHA Phenomenon. The ability of the technical names of all movie computers to improbably collapse into a cute acronym, usually a female name; e.g., "Triply-Recursive Iteratively Symbolic Hierarchical Analyzer."

ANDY IHNATKO, *Westwood, Mass.*

Tucco's Advice. Named for the character played by Eli Wallach in *The Good, the Bad and the Ugly*. It comes in the scene where Tucco is taking a bath, and a guy bursts in the room, promising Tucco he will have vengeance on him. At that moment, Tucco kills him. Tucco then advises the corpse, "If you have to shoot, shoot, don't talk." (See also Fallacy of the Talking Killer.)

STEPHEN J. BAUGHMAN

Turn It Off Rule. Immediately after the radio or TV reports something important to the plot, someone must always reach over and turn it off.

KYLE L. CAIN, *Sugar Land, Tex.*

Turning a Deaf Ear. Movie heroes squeeze off hundreds of rounds of ammo but suffer no hearing loss. For example, in *Rambo III*, Rambo enters a metal warehouse and runs an entire belt of ammo through his M-60 machine gun. Afterward he carries on a whispered conversation with the evil CIA man in another room.

JOSEPH HOLMES

Turtle Effect. Once characters are knocked down, they just lie there as if unable to get up. (Cf. Sigourney Weaver in *Alien*.)

JAMES PORTANOVA, *Fresh Meadows, N.Y.*

Two Sentence Rule. Any character who is introduced more than halfway through an action movie and (a) has a dialogue of more than two sentences with a major character, or (b) reveals to a major character that he/she has reached a milestone (twenty-first birthday, just got married, gets out of prison tomorrow, etc.) will die a tragic death before the end of the movie, cradled in the arms of that same character.

SEAN COLLINS

Unattributed Critical Quotation. Words of praise for a film, contained within quotation marks and looking exactly like an excerpt from a review, but with their source curiously missing. There is a reason for that: They do not have a source, but have been written for the occasion by a movie publicist, who hopes that since they look like quotes from real critics, a hasty reader or TV viewer will be fooled.

107

Undead Dead

Undead Dead. In horror movies, whenever the killer is killed, he is never dead. This rule is as old as the movies, but was given its modern shape in *Halloween* (1978) when the killer arose from apparent destruction to jump up behind Jamie Lee Curtis. Since then, all of the Dead Teenager Movies, most of the Bond pictures, and many other thrillers have used a false climax, in which the villain is killed—only to spring up for a final threat. In an ordinary thriller, the cliché of the Undead Dead is part of the game—but its use in *Fatal Attraction* was unforgivable.

Universal Translator. Device carried by all spaceships, allowing instantaneous translation from any alien language into the local language. The most incredible thing about this device is the way it can alter any accompanying visual transmission from the aliens. If you look closely you will see the perfect synchronization of the speaking alien's lips to the lip movements of the local language.

RICHARD ROHRDANZ, *West Kennebunk, Maine*

Universal Movie Computer Operating Laws. (1). All computers in a hi-tech movie have digitized speech and/or a personality. (2). The person typing on a computer speaks aloud what is on the screen, no matter how secret the information is. (3). Every teenage computer user is a hacker and owns a modem (cf. *WarGames*, etc.). (4). Teenage hackers use computers to pick up girls who don't have a clue about computers.

OLLI LEHTO, *Helsinki, Finland*

Unknown Team Member. Used in *Star Trek* movies, cop movies, war movies, etc., whenever a team is on a dangerous mission. The unknown team member, not a recognizable actor, will be dead within forty-five seconds. "Jones is dead, sir." is a standard epitaph.

SAM WAAS, *Houston*

Unmotivated Close-up. A character is given a close-up in a scene where there seems to be no reason for it. This is an infallible tip-off that this character is more significant than at first appears, and is most likely the killer. See the lingering close-up of the undercover KGB agent near the beginning of *The Hunt for Red October*.

STUART CLELAND, *Chicago*

Unsilenced Revolver. Despite dozens of movies which think otherwise, a revolver cannot be silenced, because the sound escapes, not from the barrel where they fit the silencer, but from the gap between the frame and the cylinder. Only closed-breech weapons, like pistols with magazines in the grip, can be silenced—unless you wrap them in a pillow.

DAWSON E. RAMBO, *Las Vegas*

Unwise Trust Movie. A new genre in which an unsuspecting baby boomer confides in a psychopathic stranger. Started in recent years by *Fatal Attraction* (casual sex), it has expanded to other areas such as tenants (*Pacific Heights*), baby-sitters (*The Hand That Rocks the Cradle*), roommates (*Single White Female*), policemen (*Unlawful Entry*), and office workers (*The Temp*).

DAVE KALIN, *San Francisco*

Waterfall Rule

Vacuum Sound Effects. Most movies set in space, with the notable exception of *2001, A Space Odyssey*, treat the viewer to a full range of sound effects. Without a medium (air) to transport the sound waves there would, of course, be no sound.

JOHN D. MCCLUSKEY

Vinny Rule. In every movie with Italian-American characters, one must be named Vinny.

DONALD MUNSCH, *Sherman, Tex.*

Voice Transplant Syndrome. Aural shock of hearing an actor lip-syncing to the voice of a better singer, when you've heard that actor sing in his/her own voice in other movies (e.g., Audrey Hepburn, who warbles in her tolerable mezzo in *Funny Face* and *Breakfast at Tiffany's*, but suddenly becomes a brilliant coloratura in *My Fair Lady*, courtesy of the singing voice of Marnie Nixo).

ANTHONY BRUCE GILPIN, *Riverside, Calif.*

"Wait Right Here!" Rule. One character, usually male, tells another character, usually female, to "Wait right here. Do *not* follow me into the warehouse, cave, house, etc." The woman inevitably does so, is captured, and must be rescued. Often inspires the line, "I thought I told you to wait outside."

DONNA A. HIGGINS, *Prairie du Chien, Wis.*

Waterfall Rule. If character falls into a river, it is inevitably just upstream of a major waterfall or series of rapids. This is true no matter how flat the terrain has been to this point or how gentle the stream. No one ever falls into a river downstream from rough water.

JOE DICOSTANZO, *New York City*

Wayne's World Rule. In any movie based on a television show, at least a quarter of the audience will be involutarily trying to change the channel.

BILL BECWAR, *Wauwatosa, Wis.*

Weak-Ankled Female Syndrome, The. Whenever a man and woman are on the run, the woman inevitably falls and sprains her ankle. As a result, the man must drag or carry her and their progress is slowed, stalled, or halted.

BRIDGETTE CLARK, *Moundsville, W. Va.*

Wedding Cake Rule. In any movie comedy involving a wedding, the cake will be destroyed.

JOHN WECKMUELLER, *Menomonie, Wis.*

We're Alive! Let's Kiss! Inevitable conclusion to any scene in which hero and heroine take cover from danger in each other's arms. (Cf. *High Road to China, Die Hard*— where Bruce Willis kisses his wife, forgetting that he is in a burning building.)

Wet Road Rule. Any road seen in a film, no matter how hot or dry the day has been, will be wet, slick, and reflecting headlights after nightfall. This is most commonly seen in deserts and drought-stricken cities like Los Angeles.

EDWARD SAVIO, *San Francisco*

Wet Star Rule. In Hollywood story conferences, suggested alternative to nude, as in: "If she won't take off her clothes, can we wet her down?" Suggested by Harry Cohn's remark about swimming star Esther Williams: "Dry, she ain't much. Wet, she's a star."

"We've Got Company." These words are always used to inform the driver of a vehicle that it is being followed by the police.

Wharton's Law. If you were forced to read the book in high school, you'll probably hate the movie, too.

ANDY IHNATKO, *Westwood, Mass.*

What Happened to Our Dreams of Changing the World? A genre first identified by Adam Mars Jones, in the *London Independent*, 1992. Examples: *Four Corners, Return of the Secaucus Seven, The Big Chill, Indian Summer, Peter's Friends.*

"What's That Supposed to Mean?" Dialogue invariably used by accused party in romantic argument. Win bets with your friends while watching made-for-TV melodramas: phrase occurs in every single one.

MICHAEL J. PILLING, *Maple Ridge, B.C., Canada*

Wild Kingdom Phenomenon. No interesting animal is limited to its natural range. This mismatching probably started with Tarzan films, in which Tarzan rode Asian elephants, fought tigers (Asia only) and cougars (Americas only), wrestled American alligators, and avoided boa constrictors (tropical America only).

STEVE W. ZACK

Willis Duct. In all movies about a lone hero who battles terrorists on a boat/building/plane, there is always one duct which doesn't appear on the terrorists' copy of the blueprints but which the hero immediately locates and uses to escape from the floor/deck/room where the terrorists think the hero is trapped and can do no harm.

ANDY IHNATKO, *Westwood, Mass.*

Windows of the Soul. Any main character who wears glasses will, at least once, take the glasses off to express some deep emotion or give an impassioned speech.

JERRY RITCEY

Women's Shower Syndrome. Movies with scenes set in women's showers inevitably portray them as brightly lit, open playrooms where nude women laugh, frolic, and snap each other with towels. Those not participating in high jinks are slowly and seductively soaping themselves under the shower spray.

JAMES MOORE, *San Jose, Calif.*

Wrongheaded Commanding Officer. In modern police movies, the commanding officer exists solely for the purpose of taking the hero off the case, calling him on the carpet, issuing dire warnings, asking him to hand over his badge and gun, etc. (Cf. the Dirty Harry series, *Blue Steel*, etc.)

TONY WHITEHOUSE, *Verbier, Switzerland*

Wunza Movie. Any film using a plot which can be summarized by saying "One's a . . ." For example, "One's a cop. One's an actor." Or "One's a saint. One's a sinner."

DAVID KING, *Los Angeles*

X-Ray Driver. In many thrillers, the hero crashes his car or truck through the window or wall of a building at the precise time and place to allow him to rescue a victim or kill the bad guys. How can he see through the walls to know exactly where his car will emerge? Why doesn't he ever drive into a load-bearing beam?

Yakima Canute Rule. Any chase scene involving a fistfight between the hero and bad guys while they are speeding in a truck or wagon requires the hero to fall over the front of the vehicle, slide between the wheels to the rear, and pull himself up onto the back, surprising the bad guys. (Named after the famous stunt man who originated this move in stagecoach chase scenes.)

SAM WAAS, *Houston*

Youngblood Rule. No movie with a hero named "Youngblood" has ever been any good. (Cf. *Youngblood Hawke, Youngblood*, etc.)

"You've Got to Believe Me!" Rule. The character who is seeing and hearing things is invariably the only one who knows what is really going on.

BENJAMIN JOHNSON, *Provo, Utah*

Z. Pronounced "zed" in British movies, something most American audiences do not know.